EXPLAINING THE GOSPELS

Explaining
the Gospels

by

Wilfrid J. Harrington, O.P.

PAULIST PRESS

NEW YORK / PARAMUS, N. J.

A Deus Books Edition of the Paulist Press, 1963, by special arrangement with Dominican Publications, Dublin.

For Chapters I - VI:

NIHIL OBSTAT: Fr. Ailbeus Ryan, O.P., S.T.L.
Fr. Richardus MacLoughlin, O.P., S.T.L., L.S.S.
IMPRIMI POTEST: Fr. Ludovicus C. Coffey, O.P.
Provincialis.
die 20 Octobris, 1961.
NIHIL OBSTAT: Fr. Ambrosius M. Crofts, O.P., S.T.L., M.A.
Censor Theol. Deput.
IMPRIMI POTEST: ✠ Joannes Carolus
Archiep. Dublinen., Hiberniae Primas:
Dublini, die 30 Octobris, 1961.

For Chapters VII - XII:

NIHIL OBSTAT: Fr. Guillelmus Barden, O.P., S.T.M.
Fr. Richardus MacLoughlin, O.P., S.T.L., L.S.S.
IMPRIMI POTEST: Fr. Ludovicus C. Coffey, O.P.
Provincialis.
die 15 Novembris, 1961.
NIHIL OBSTAT: Fr. Ambrosius M. Crofts, O.P., S.T.L., M.A.
Censor Theol. Deput.
IMPRIMI POTEST: ✠ Joannes Carolus
Archiep. Dublinen., Hiberniae Primas:
Dublini, die 23 Novembris, 1961.

For Chapters XIII - XVII:

NIHIL OBSTAT: Fr. Guillelmus Barden, O.P., S.T.M.
Fr. Richardus MacLoughlin, O.P., S.T.L., L.S.S.
IMPRIMI POTEST: Fr. Ludovicus C. Coffey, O.P.
Provincialis.
die 30 Januarii, 1962
NIHIL OBSTAT: Fr. Ambrosius M. Crofts, O.P., S.T.L., M.A.
Censor Theol. Deput.
IMPRIMI POTEST: ✠ Joannes Carolus
Archiep. Dublinen., Hiberniae Primas:
Dublini, die 7 Februarii, 1962.

Contents

5

Contents

Preface

The Bible is still very much a closed book to the majority of Catholics and, to a certain extent, this is inevitable. No one can hope to understand the Old Testament without some preparation, and any version of the sacred books meant for layfolk ought to provide adequate helps. The New Testament, too, has its difficulties, but its atmosphere is more familiar to us. Indeed, anybody can read the gospels at least. Not everything will be clear, but there is much that is simple and straightforward: the miracles of our Lord, his teaching and, above all, the poignant story of his Passion.

We can profit from all this, yet unless we know how to read the gospels intelligently, appreciating something of their true character, we cannot savor their full richness. It is quite likely that as we get more familiar with them we will be perplexed and perhaps scandalized by the difficulties that spring up. We will not know what to make of these and we may feel tempted to drop our scriptural reading altogether, or confine ourselves to a few familiar and 'safe' passages. That would be a pity.

Yet, one can sympathize with this attitude. Though today the gospels are better understood than ever before—by Scripture scholars—the average Catholic has no clearer understanding of them. It is unfortunate that this is the case and there is no valid reason why it should be so. The fact is that our method of teaching Scripture in schools has not kept pace with recent progress, and most manuals and introductions that lay people might use are hopelessly dated.

There used to be overmuch emphasis—indeed exclusive emphasis—on apologetics, and we have not yet quite rid ourselves of this outlook. Difficulties and disturbing facts are still frequently ignored or explained away. The trouble is that the reader becomes aware of these difficulties, and he is not very impressed by many of the arguments that seek to dispose of them. There is, in fact, no justification for a negative, almost diffident, attitude towards Scripture, for Catholic biblical scholarship is no longer on the defensive but is very sure of itself. It is making constant progress on its own and it is willing, too, to accept contributions from every side, even from quarters that at first seem most unpromising.

Any introduction to the gospels that would fail to take full cognizance of the work of our present-day Catholic exegetes would be an insult to these scholars. It would be contrary to the mind of Pope Pius XII as it is expressed clearly and forcibly in his encyclical *Divino Afflante Spiritu*. It would, moreover, be an injustice to our Catholic laity by depriving them of the light that could illuminate the gospels for them. The gospels are the heritage of all Christians, and all should be given the opportunity of knowing and understanding them better.

In this book I have made an attempt to meet a real need, and it is hoped that this modest introduction will be of help to those who are anxious to gain a deeper insight into the gospels. It has in view readers who have had no scriptural or theological training, but it does demand of them a certain effort. Though the appearance of a text book has been avoided, it really is a text book in the sense that it must be studied and not just read; there is no easy way to understanding the gospels. But I trust that any effort expended will be rewarded and, with this in mind, I have been careful to avoid questions that do not contribute to a deeper grasp of the subject.

I believe that even an elementary introduction, such as this, must still be up-to-date, and I have striven to make it so. The outlook throughout is positive and, since my intention is to open the way to a real understanding of the gospels, the positive approach is the only justifiable one. Scripture study is not an exercise in apologetics—it is a seeking after the words of eternal life. For that reason a large place has been given to a study of the method of the evangelists and to an explanation of the outstanding theological ideas of their writings, because this is the only way to the true meaning of the gospels and to the discernment of their message. I can only hope that this little work will, for some at least, be the first step towards a fuller and richer appreciation of the Good News.

WILFRID J. HARRINGTON, O.P.

I

Behind the Gospels

1. Origin of the Gospels

The gospels tell us of Christ and his teaching—but they were not written by him. Jesus did not describe such and such a miracle, he worked it. Jesus suffered and died and rose again, he did not give an account of these. The same is true of his teaching. His sayings and parables were spoken bv him, but they were written down by others; they have come to us not as he spoke them, but as others remembered them. They may have been remembered and recorded exactly as he spoke them, and they may not; an examination of the gospels shows us that we must consider this second alternative. So we must turn to the evangelists.

The gospels were written by the four evangelists, but these wrote many years after the Resurrection, after the events they relate. We must not imagine that they wrote the gospels out of their heads, relying only on what they had seen and heard and remembered. We have only to recall that St. Mark was not an Apostle and that St. Luke was certainly not a disciple in order to realize that these, at least, must have been dependent on others, St. Luke altogether and St. Mark to a large extent. But quite apart from that, it is now clear that the evangelists set about their task in a perfectly natural way by making use of such accounts or documents as served their purpose.

We must go beyond the evangelists because, though they have given us a fourfold account of the Good News, they themselves are not the authors of the Good News; they have put the story of our Lord in writing, but that story existed long before they wrote. Between Christ and the evangelists come the Apostles, the Church. Thus we get back, ultimately, to the early Church, for it was the Church, represented by the Apostles, that drew up the original gospel which was afterwards handed on to us, according to the viewpoint of each, by the four evangelists.

We have three stages, then: Jesus Christ, the Church and the evangelists. It is only when we take all these into account that we can really hope to understand the gospels, and in the light of this realization many apparent problems are seen to be no problems at all. We must have noticed, for example, that the evangelists rarely agree verbatim, even when reporting sayings of our Lord and, indeed, there are some very notable differences. That they do differ so may surprise us, but, rather, it is just what we should expect. They are true authors, writing with a definite purpose in mind and, too, they often owe their information to sources that are not always identical. It is to be hoped that this book will help us to realize these facts; for, otherwise, we can never get a really intelligent grasp of the gospels.

2. Gospel

The Greek word for gospel is *euangelion,* whence the Latin *evangelium.* (Our "gospel" is from early English god spel = "good news.") In the early Church *euangelion* signified, not a book dealing with the words and works of Christ, but, rather, the Good News of Messianic salvation, the message of salvation. The word was already found in the Greek translation of the Old Testament. For example, we read in Isaias: "How beautiful upon the mountains are the feet of him who announces *good tidings*—the message of peace, who announces *good tidings* of good" 52, 7. The word is the same, but in the Old Testament the good news is that of future salvation, whereas the gospels are the good news of a salvation that has been achieved.

The gospel may be the Good News that Christ himself preached (e.g., Mark 1, 15; Matt. 11, 5; Luke 4, 18); or it may be the apostolic preaching concerning Christ and the salvation that is found in him (e.g. Acts 5, 42; Rom 1, 1f.). It comes to the same thing because always it is a question of Christ and his teaching. We should note that it is a matter of "preaching," not of the written word, and Christian missionaries are called "evangelists" (Acts 21, 8; Eph 4, 11; II Tim 4, 5). We must realize that in the New Testament itself the word "gospel" means the *preaching* of Christ, and the "evangelist" is a *preacher*.

But words often change, and, frequently, a word that has quite a broad meaning acquires a precise technical sense. So it was that in the second century *euangelion* came to designate the written account of the life and teaching of our Lord, and it was at the same time, too, that the authors of the gospels were called evangelists. Thus we should keep in mind that our very special meaning for "gospel" and "evangelist" is not quite that of the New Testament itself. There is no contradiction, of course, but since the terminology does occur in scripture, it is well to be aware of its development.

3. Oral Tradition

Before the gospels were written they were preached. This is quite obvious—when we advert to it. If the evangelists, particularly the first three evangelists (St. Matthew, St. Mark and St. Luke) do differ in some respects, yet they agree in giving more or less the same teaching of our Lord and in telling us much the same things about him. There would be nothing strange in this if they had told us *all* that he had said and *all* that he did. This, obviously is not so, and St. John was very well aware of it (John 21, 25). But if it is patent that they tell us only very few of the things he did, and that they give us but a very small part of his preaching, then it is clear that they could not all have chosen just the same events and sayings quite independently.

The very first problem that confronted the Apostles when they set about their task of preaching Christ was how to present that message. If each of them, and each of the disciples, were to preach what had struck him about the Lord, and the words of the Lord that each had remembered, those to whom they preached would have been utterly confused. There had to be organization from the start. For practical missionary purposes a selection had to be made from the deeds and sayings of Christ, and that task clearly fell to the Apostles under the leadership of Peter.

We learn from the early chapters of the *Acts of the Apostles* that, after Pentecost, Peter was the principal witness of Christ. In his preaching he traced the main lines of the public life of Christ, always after a definite pattern. (Cf. Acts 1, 21-22; 2, 22-24; 10, 37-41.) This order is at the basis of the first three gospels; it falls into four main divisions:

(i) Preparation and Baptism in Judea, i.e., the preaching of John the Baptist and the inauguration of the public ministry of Christ. (ii) Ministry in Galilee. (iii) Journey from Galilee to Jerusalem. (iv) In Jerusalem: Passion, Death, Resurrection.

The last part, the Passion-narrative, was the first to take shape—this is attested by the close parallelism of all four gospels. The other details from the life of our Lord and many of his sayings were added so that the gospels have been described, not unjustly, as "Passion-narratives with an introduction." It is certainly apparent that the most remarkable thing about Christ, in the eyes of the early Church, was his Death and Resurrection.

It is important to realize from the beginning that in the process of presenting the Good News according to this fourfold division and within this framework, the life and ministry of our Lord have been considerably simplified. If we had only the first three gospels we might have thought that the ministry of Christ lasted less than a year. Only one Pasch is mentioned, that of the Passion, so, apparently, he would have begun his work sometime after the same feast of the previous year. It would appear, too, that during his ministry, he visited Jerusalem once only, on the journey to his death. But we have a fourth gospel, and St. John makes it clear that the ministry of our Lord lasted more than two

years—he mentions three Paschs.[1] He tells us, too, that
Christ visited Jerusalem frequently, and preached there at
length.

Obviously, both of these presentations cannot be historically accurate. But we must not now jump to the conclusion that we are confronted by a plain contradiction in the
gospels. At the same time we cannot evade the difficulty
merely by asserting, dogmatically, that there is no contradiction. There is a reasonable explanation.

The gospel of St. John will be studied in it own time,
but we can take it that his view of the longer ministry of
our Lord is historical. The other gospels are much more
closely attached to the original preaching, and follow more
nearly the plan drawn up by the Apostles. We have seen
that this original plan was devised with catechetical interests
in view. There had to be agreement on the selection of the
events of our Lord's life and of points from his teaching;
an inevitable result was simplification, schematization.

Let us consider just the events of our Savior's life. We
have noted that the death and resurrection are central, and
this event was first considered. But on a broader view it
was seen that our Lord was preceded by one who had come
to prepare the way for him—something had to be said
about John the Baptist; he was the first herald of the Good
News, but when Christ appeared his task was finished. The
baptism of Jesus, not only in fact, but very conveniently
too, brought him and John together and thus dramatically
introduced the public ministry. This is indeed the beginning
of the gospel.[2] After this our Lord carried out his mission
in Galilee. Accounts of his journeys and of his miracles
were grouped with records or typical teaching of his, and
even isolated sayings. The journey of Christ to his death is
all the more dramatic because it is presented as his only
entry into Jerusalem.

The framework is conventional but there is no falsification of historical facts because, in this respect, the intention
is not primarily historical. We are not being presented with
a biography of Jesus and there is no real interest in chronology. Yet the plan does correspond to an historical and
theological reality. Christ was at first very favorably re-

ceived by the people, but his humble and spiritual Messianism disappointed their hopes and their enthusiasm waned. Then he withdrew from Galilee to devote himself to the formation of a little group of faithful disciples. He won their unconditional support after Peter's confession of faith at Caesarea Philippi. That was a decisive turning-point: the road now led to Jerusalem. In the face of mounting opposition the drama of the Passion was played out; but seeming failure was turned into triumph by the Resurrection.

This is the reality, at once theological and historical, which lies behind the plan of the apostolic preaching. It is not concerned with giving a detailed biography of Christ —this is an entirely modern idea. But it has given the essentials, there is no falsification. From the first three gospels it would appear that the public ministry lasted less than a year; that is no more than an impression—it is nowhere asserted that this was so. One might come to that conclusion because one did not understand the methods and intentions of those who drew up the tradition. The object was to show the ministry of the Messiah from its favorable beginning in Galilee to the tragedy in Jerusalem, and the gospels do bring home to us that historical process.

For us moderns, the time element, a detailed chronology, would be an obvious part of any such presentation. But does the duration of the ministry of Christ really affect the purpose and the importance and the effects of that ministry? Is not the question of chronology very secondary indeed? The early converts knew and believed that the Son of God had preached to men and had suffered and died. That is all they needed to know, and surely it is enough.

So far we have considered events only. When we turn to the sayings we find that, on the whole, the same sayings of our Lord are recorded by the three evangelists—though Mark has very much less of these than Matthew and Luke. But rarely do we find that any saying occurs, in identical form, in any two gospels. Generally, the differences are insignificant, but frequently enough they are more far-reaching.

Again we must view this problem in perspective. It

would be unreasonable to expect to have the words of our Lord always recorded in just the same way. Indeed, it is impossible to have any sayings of his *exactly* as they came from his lips, for the very good reason that he spoke Aramaic (a Semitic language akin to Hebrew) and our gospels were written in Greek. What we have is a translation of the sayings of our Lord, and a translation does not have to be slavishly literal. A saying or passage can be rendered quite faithfully in more than one form by using synonymous terms, and stylistic changes will not alter the sense. This explains many of the variations that we discern in sayings of Christ in the gospels.

But there are more serious differences and, not infrequently, where we should least expect them. Matthew and Mark agree closely in their account of the institution of the Eucharist (Matt. 26, 26-28; Mark 14, 22-24), whereas Luke has a different version even of the words of institution (22, 19-20). Matthew has nine beatitudes (5, 3-12) and Luke has four, with the addition of four parallel "woes" (6, 20-26). Matthew's version of the Lord's Prayer (6, 9-13) has seven petitions, while Luke's version has five only (11, 2-4). Mark omits altogether the Sermon on the Mount; Matthew gives a long account of it (5, 1-7, 29), and Luke's form is notably shorter.

We cannot ignore such differences, but there is no need to be perturbed by them. However, unless we understand very clearly how the gospels have been written, we shall be quite unable to give a reasonable explanation of such facts. For the divergencies can be satisfactorily explained, but only if various factors are taken into account and each is given its due weight. For the moment it is enough to have indicated these divergencies; we now go on to consider the general principles that lead to a solution of the problem.

An oral tradition lies behind our gospels. This does not merely mean that the gospel message was first preached, or merely that it was cast in a definite mold, from the beginning. It means, too, that we can, in our gospels, still discern traces of that oral tradition. The first preachers and teachers were at pains to ensure that the gospel message should be retained and so the episodes and sayings were, as far as possible, presented in a way that could be easily remembered. We can still identify some of these forms, and as we study them we can see the gospel taking shape before our eyes. We get back to the very origin of the gospels and, in the case of sayings, we approach as closely as possible to our Lord himself.

We know from experience that it is easier to remember verse than prose; it used to be a feature of pedagogy that grammatical rules, and suchlike, were cast in rough verses. We find the same method in the gospels. Thus rhythm—an essential feature of poetry—and parallelism, which is distinctive of Hebrew poetry, are quite in evidence. It will be helpful to study some examples of the "oral style." This is not a matter merely of curiosity, for quite apart from the fact that we are brought back to the earliest stages of the tradition, a realization of these factors will help our interpretation of many gospel passages. We can see this, for instance, in the case of the keywords mentioned below.

(i) *Rhythm.* In the Old Testament writings rhythm is largely present in the psalms and prophetical books. The parallel with the prophetical writings is particularly instructive because these were precisely the parts of the Old Testament which were first pronounced in public before being written down. We should expect to find traces of rhythm in the sayings of our Lord, e.g., Matt. 6, 9-13; 7, 17; Mark 7, 8. A striking example is Matt. 16, 17-19. Here we give an English translation of a Greek text that is itself based on an Aramaic original.[*] Even at third hand the balance and rhythm are obvious; surely we are very close to the accents of Christ.

The passage consists of three verses, each verse contains three lines and each line is divided into two balanced parts:

> Blessed are you / Simon Bar-Jona!
> for flesh and blood / has not revealed to you,
> but my Father / in the heavens.

> And I say to you / that you are Rock (Peter)
> and on this rock / I will build my Church
> and the gates of hell / shall not prevail against it.

I shall give you the keys / of the kingdom of heaven,
and whatever you bind on earth / shall be bound in
heaven,
and whatever you loose on earth / shall be loosed in
heaven.

(ii) *Parallelism.* Here again we have a feature that is
prominent in the psalms and prophetical literature; it is
distinctive of Hebrew poetry. The different types of parallelism are represented in the sayings of Christ.

Synonymous parallelism: Where the two members of a
couplet express the same idea; the second renders the sense
of the first in different words. E.g.,

He who receives a prophet because he is a prophet
shall receive a prophet's reward;
and he who receives a just man because he is a just
man
shall receive a just man's reward. Matt. 10, 41.

Everyone to whom much is given, of him will much
be required;
and of him to whom men commit much they will
demand the more. Luke 12, 48.

Antithetical parallelism: Where the terms of the second
member contrast with those of the first. E.g.,

The sabbath was made for man,
not man for the sabbath. Mark 2, 27. Cf. Matt. 7, 17;
Luke 12, 47-48.

Progressive parallelism: Where the sense of the first
member is developed in the second. E.g.,

He who receives you receives me,
and he who receives me receives him who sent me.
Matt. 10, 40. Cf. Mark 9, 37; Luke 12, 4-5.

All three types can be found in the passage Matt. 10, 39-41.

These examples show us that our Lord deliberately cast his sayings into forms that are redolent of the Old Testament, but more important still, they thereby become more easily remembered; we are close to the very words of Jesus. The following elements of the "oral style" are the work of the Church.

(iii) *Schematization,* i.e., narrative episodes are often built on the same model, after a very simple plan. Miracle stories, especially, are stripped down to the essentials and appear in a stereotyped form. E.g., in Mark the casting out of an evil spirit and the stilling of a tempest are related in almost identical terms: 1, 25-27 and 4, 39-41. Cf. 7, 32-37 and 8, 22-26; 11, 1-6 and 14, 13-16.

(iv) *Mnemonic aids,* i.e., sayings are joined together by a system of key words. E.g., 18, 1-35; Mark 9, 33-50; Luke 9, 46-50. In this passage what appears at first sight to be a continuous discourse turns out to be a collection of isolated sayings. The process is clearest in Mark. In v. 35 the word "servant" occurs and in the following verse the word "child." The underlying key word is *talya,* the Aramaic for both "servant" and "child"—and we have a typically Semitic wordplay, such as occurs frequently in the Old Testament. In v. 37 there is question of receiving a child "in the name of" Jesus and in the next verse John refers to one who cast out devils "in the name of" Christ; clearly the phrase "in the name of" is the only link between these verses. The word "name" appears again in v. 41 but in a different context. In v. 42 "child" reappears and then the theme of "scandal" is developed. A close study of the three parallel texts reveals that behind them lies a group of sayings linked together by seven key words; it is a system for remembering different sayings of our Lord. it is important that such groups should be recognized for what they are, for then we will not be perturbed by a lack of logical sequence and, consequently, not a few misinterpretations can be avoided.

Another mnemonic aid is the *inclusion*—found in Hebrew and Aramaic. It is a sort of refrain, arranged in such a way that a discourse, which may be quite short, begins and ends with the same word or words, or with the same idea. The passage in question is thus clearly marked off as a unit.

E.g., Matt. 5, 3b. 10b; 7, 16a. 20; 15, 2.20; 16, 6.12; 19, 30. 20, 16. (This form can very well go back to our Lord, in some cases at least.)

4. Primitive Literary Units

We have seen so far that the apostolic Church gave the gospel story its shape. The Passion, Death and Resurrection form the central part, and the events were chosen to show the development from the beginning of the public ministry to Calvary. But the discourses and sayings of our Lord were also selected. Very often sayings were preserved becaused they solved some pressing problem, or pointed the way to a particular line of conduct. We have seen some traces of the oral style; we can also identify many of the literary units which stand behind the gospels and which took shape within the Church.

Some of these forms go back to our Lord himself—the parables are an obvious example. Others are due to the Church. Christ worked miracles, but it is the Apostles who first told of them, and so we get miracle stories. It is the Church, too, which composed Pronouncement Stories, in which a narrative leads up to and concentrates on a saying or pronouncement of Christ:

And they sent to him some of the Pharisees and some of the Herodians, to entrap him in his talk. They came and said to him: "Master, we know that you are candid and are no respecter of persons; for you do not regard the rank of men, but teach with all candor the way of God. Is it lawful to pay taxes to Caesar? Should we or should we not pay?" But he, knowing their hypocrisy, said to them: "Why do you put me to the test? Bring me a denarius and let me look at it." And he said to them: "Whose image and inscription is this?" They said to him: "Caesar's." Jesus said to them: "Render to Caesar the things that are Caesar's and to God the things that are God's." And they were amazed at him. Mark 12, 13-17.

It is evident that the narrative builds up to a climax; it is the saying that matters and the details only serve to set it in relief. The relation of Church and State, the clash of civil and religious interests, is nothing new. The early Christians had to face this problem, and that is why the saying of our Lord was remembered and treasured.

We must be careful how we evaluate the various literary units that lie behind the gospels. It is quite true that the gospels are not biographies of Jesus. It is true that the gospel elements are frequently joined together in no strict chronological or geographical order, and they are often linked by only the most tenuous literary ties. Nevertheless, there is a real unity, for the component parts, all the words and deeds, center around Jesus, the Messiah who had come. Then, too, each of the evangelists is an author, not a mere compiler. The three gospels are personal works, each having its own definite stamp and character—they are far from being mosaics of disparate fragments, as some would regard them. Neither the evangelists nor the early Christians were interested in producing a biography of Christ according to our modern standards, but that does not render their work unhistorical. "The early Christians had not, perhaps, our regard for 'history,' but they had regard for the 'historical.' The preachers of the new faith did not intend to relate *everything* about Jesus, but they were careful to relate only what was solidly founded." [4]

The Church did not create the gospel in the sense that it invented it, yet it obviously is responsible for much of it. It composed the narrative parts, and the needs and interests of the Church did influence the selection of the sayings of our Lord. This creative activity is mainly concerned with the literary forms into which the traditional data were cast, but it is not limited to these. There was, too, a cerain amount of interpretation and adaptation. It would be false to the words of Christ when he promised to send the Holy Spirit on his disciples, if their role were limited to a mechanical passing on of his teaching: "The Paraclete, the

Holy Spirit, whom the Father will send in my name, he will teach you all things, and recall to your mind all that I have said to you." John 14, 26. Cf. 16, 13. It is evident from the gospels and the early chapters of Acts, that the Apostles needed more than a recollection of the words of Jesus. It is only after the Resurrection that they really understood Christ, and the account of Pentecost dramatically shows how the coming of the Holy Spirit enlightened them. Not until then were their eyes fully opened. Not until then could the gospel have been written.

II

The Synoptic Problem

The first three gospels are closely related—St. John goes his own way. The narratives and discourses of Matthew, Mark and Luke have common or corresponding passages which may be arranged in parallel columns. Thus one gets a double or triple form of the same gospel event or saying, and one may see at a glance, and in detail, the resemblances and differences. The text so arranged is called by the Greek term *synopsis* = "seeing together." Hence we get the name "Synoptics" applied since the end of the eighteenth century to the first three gospels.[1]

The following texts will illustrate what we mean, and will give an indication of the complexity of the problem.

(1) A QUESTION ABOUT FASTING.

Matt. 9, 15-15.	Mark 2, 18-20.	Luke 5, 33-35.
Then the disciples of John	Now the disciples of John and the Pharisees were fasting,	
approached him saying:	and people came and said to him:	And they said to him:
Why do we	Why do the disciples of John	The disciples of John fast often

and the Pharisees fast	and the disciples of the Pharisees fast	and offer prayers and so do those of the Pharisees,
but your disciples do not fast? And Jesus said to them: Can the children of the wedding-feast (2) mourn as long as the bridegroom is with them?	but your disciples do not fast? And Jesus said to them: Can the children of the wedding-feast fast while the bridegroom is with them? As long as they have the bridegroom with them they cannot fast.	but yours eat and drink. but Jesus said to them: Can you make the children of the wedding - feast fast while the bridegroom is with them?
The days will come when the bridegroom will be taken away from them and then they will fast.	The days will come when the bridegroom will be taken away from them and then they will fast in that day.	The days will come and when the bridegroom will be taken away from them— then they will fast in those days.

(2) IN THE SYNAGOGUE AT CAPHARNAUM.

Mark 1, 23-28.	Luke 33-37.
And then there was in their synagogue a man with an unclean spirit and he cried out, saying:	And there was in the synagogue a man who had the spirit of an impure devil and he cried out in a loud voice:
What is your business with us Jesus the Nazarene? Have you come to destroy us? we know who you are, the Holy One of God. Jesus rounded on him, "Hold your tongue," he said, "and come out of the man." And the unclean spirit con-	Ha! what is your business with us Jesus the Nazarene? Have you come to destroy us. we know who you are, the Holy One of God. Jesus rounded on him, "Hold your tongue." he said "and come out of the man." And the demon flung him into

vulsed the man, gave a loud cry and came out of him.	their midst and without having done him any harm came out of him.
And all were amazed as they questioned one another, saying: what is this? a new doctrine with authority! He even commands unclean spirits	And amazement fell on all and they discussed among themselves, saying: what is this thing?, for he commands unclean spirits with authority and power
and they obey him. From that moment his fame spread everywhere through all the countryside of Galilee.	and they come out! And his renown spread into every part of the countryside.

The relationship between the Synoptics is a strange combination of agreement and disagreement, and it pervades the gospels in such a way that there are variations in important matters and perfect accord in mere details. This fact, and the problem it raises, is not just academic. No attempted solution has been generally accepted, but the discussion of the problem, and the indication of the lines along which the solution must lie, are of real help in understanding the gospels. We shall first consider, briefly, the agreement between the gospels and then their differences. It is recommended that a copy of the New Testament should be at hand and the references should be looked up.

1. Agreements

The main lines of the gospel story are the same in all three narratives. Similarly, the rare geographical and chronological indications are the same: the appearance of John the Baptist and the manifestation of Christ; the preaching in Galilee and by the lake of Tiberias; the journey to Jerusalem; the Passion, Death and Resurrection. The following should be noted:

(1) The similarity between the three narratives is particularly striking in the case of certain important facts in the life of Christ: the baptism, controversies with the opponents, the multiplication of loaves, the confession of

Peter, the foretelling of the Passion, the last days in Jerusalem, the arrest, judgment and death of the Savior.

(2) In general, the elements of the gospel story are arranged in the same order in the three Synoptics. In many instances the episodes of the history follow on one another and are linked in an identical manner in the three narratives. E.g., the paralytic of Capharaum, the call of Levi, the question of fasting: Matt. 9, 1-17; Mark 2, 1-22; Luke 5, 17-39.

The calming of the storm, the demoniac of Gerasa, the daughter of Jairus: Matt. 8, 18-9, 34; Mark 4, 35-5, 43; Luke 8, 22-56.

The confession of Peter, first prediction of the Passion, the Transfiguration, the cure of an epileptic, the second prediction of the Passion, Matt. 16, 13-17, 23; Mark 8, 27-9, 32; Luke 9, 18-45.

It is obvious that such an accord cannot be fortuitous.

(3) The literary form. Even a quick examination of the parallel texts shows that frequently the expression is almost identical and that the differences in style and vocabulary are insignificant. E.g.,

The ears on the sabbath:
   Matt. 12, 1-4;   Mark   2, 23-26; Luke   6, 1-4.
The grain of mustard-seed:
   Matt. 13, 31-32; Mark   4, 30-32; Luke 13, 18-19.
The rich young man:
   Matt. 19, 16-26; Mark 10, 17-27; Luke 18, 18-27.

(4) Old Testament Citations. Sometimes there is perfect agreement in the form of an Old Testament citation found in the Synoptics even when the form is that of a version somewhat different from the Hebrew and accepted Greek translation.

In conclusion we repeat that such agreement cannot be the result of chance; the contacts are too numerous and the agreement is too marked and continuous. We shall see that the phenomenon can be explained on the grounds of interdependence among the gospels.

2. Differences

The agreement between parallel texts is manifest. On the other hand there are differences that are no less marked and no less characteristic.

(1) Sayings of Christ. Here one would expect a high degree of conformity. In fact, the disagreements are sometimes disconcerting.

Classic examples are:

The Lord's Prayer: Matt. 6, 9-13; Luke 11, 2-4.

Institution of the Eucharist: Matt. 26, 26-28; Mark 14, 22-24; Luke 22, 19-20.

(2) The elements of the gospel story.

Matthew and Luke alone give an account of the Birth and Infancy, but independently.

Mark only has the parable of the Seed Growing Secretly.

Matthew only—the Cockle, Hidden Treasure, Precious Pearl, Leaven, Net, Unjust Steward.

Luke only—The Prodigal Son, Good Samaritan, Pharisee and Publican, Rich Man and Lazarus.

(3) The order of events and discourses:

Matthew: Sermon on the Mount, chs. 5-7.

Mark: omits it.

Luke: has most of the material found in Matt. 5-7 distributed throughout Chs. 6, 11, 13, 14, 16.

Luke is independent of Matthew-Mark in 9, 51-18, 14.

Luke is in perfect accord with Mark in 4, 31-6, 19; 8, 4-9, 50; 18, 15-21, 38.

(4) The Passion narrative is essentially the same in the three Synoptics, yet there are notable differences:

Matt. 27, 46; Mark 15, 34—one word of Christ from the Cross. Luke 23, 34.43.46—gives three others and omits that of Matt.-Mark. Matt. 28, 16-20; Mark 16, 6-7—The risen Christ appears in Galilee. Luke 24, 13-53—The risen Christ appears in Jerusalem only. Matt. 27, 62-66; 28, 11-20—He alone mentions guards at the Tomb. Luke 24, 13-35—He alone mentions the disciples at Emmaus.

The explanation of these facts and of this strange relationship constitutes the Synoptic Problem. An immense amount has been written on the question since it came into prominence in the nineteenth century. The discussion of this problem has greatly contributed to a better understanding of the three gospels.

3. Toward a Solution[8]

We have seen that an oral tradition lies behind our gospels, but its influence has to be carefully measured. Attempts have been made to explain the complicated relations between the Synoptics by recourse to the stereotyped form of the gospel preaching, but these attempts have necessarily failed. There was simplification and schematization, that is undoubted, but not to the extent and in such detail as would account for the highly complicated situation that exists. Our gospels were composed a relatively long time after the primitive apostolic preaching in Palestine. Oral tradition plays its part, but literary criticism of the Synoptics shows that these must have had common *written* sources.

However, we must start from the oral tradition which, in general, is the gospel plan drawn up by the Apostles. It was composed in Aramaic, the language of our Lord and the Apostles. But even in Jerusalem there were Jews who had come from other parts of the Roman empire; such were the "Greeks" or Hellenists of Acts 6, from among whom the seven deacons were chosen. These Jews were Greek-speaking, and so the first catechesis or teaching must have appeared in Greek, too, almost from the beginning. It is natural that the oral tradition was soon, in part at least, written down; there is yet no question of a gospel, but some of the writings may have been quite long. St. Luke tells us: "Many have undertaken to write an account of these events" (1, 1). Just like the tradition, these accounts must have appeared both in Aramaic and in Greek.

A gospel, written in Aramaic, is traditionally attributed to the Apostle St. Matthew. Literary criticism has, within limits, traced the extent of this writing which is one of the main sources of our gospels; it was, essentially, a schematized form of the Palestinian catechesis, the apostolic gospel preaching. It was soon translated into Greek, and on the authority of Papias (bishop of Hierapolis in Asia Minor c. 130) we know that there were many Greek versions.[4]

A study of Matthew and Luke makes it clear that for much of their material these must have had a special source in common. This appears to have been a supplement to the Aramaic gospel of Matthew and, like it, it must have been soon translated into Greek. So, at this stage, we have various Greek translations of the Aramaic gospel of Matthew, as well as translations of a supplement to it which contained, for the most part, sayings and parables of our Lord.

And now we come to the first of the gospels as we know them. This is not Matthew, as we might have expected, but Mark. The gospel of Mark is the earliest of the gospels as they have come down to us.[5] St. Mark was not an Apostle, an eyewitness, so he followed closely a Greek translation of the Aramaic gospel of Matthew. The gospel of Mark is noted for the vivid details and lifelike touches that abound in it. (Compare Mark 2, 1-12 with Matt. 9, 1-8; Mark 4, 35-41 with Matt. 8, 23-27.) Tradition tells us that St. Mark was a disciple of St. Peter, and in that fact we have a ready explanation of these details that could have come only from an eyewitness.

Next comes the gospel of St. Matthew. It is, naturally, based primarily on a Greek translation of the Aramaic gospel. But it also makes use of Mark and of the supplementary source common to it and to Luke. Lastly, we have the gospel of Luke—though, in fact, since Matthew and Luke are quite independent it is not possible to say which has really preceded the other. This gospel is based first of all on Mark, then on a Greek translation of the Aramaic gospel of Matthew and on the source common to it and to Matthew. Both Matthew and Luke also have material, such as the Infancy narratives, which has come to them from other sources, ultimately from the oral tradition.

It may be helpful to present these data in the form of a plan.

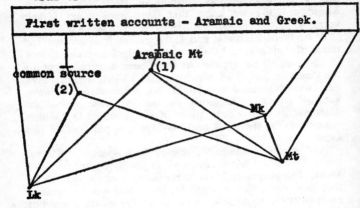

Oral tradition – Aramaic and Greek.   (Peter).

First written accounts – Aramaic and Greek.

Aramaic Mt
(1)

common source
(2)

Mk

Mt

Lk

(1) = Greek translations of Aramaic Matthew.
(2) = Greek translations of the Source Common to Matthew-Luke.

Mark is dependent on: (1) and oral tradition (via Peter).
Matthew is dependent on: (1), Mark, (2), other material from oral tradition.
Luke is dependent on: Mark, (1), (2), other material from oral tradition.

The Synoptic Problem is a complicated one and we should not expect to find for it a simple and ready solution. The theory sketched above does measure up to the difficulties and does give a reasonable explanation both of agreements and of differences between the gospels, and it does make full use both of a close literary study of the gospels and of all the traditional data. The sources of the three gospels are, in the main, the same, but they may have differed fairly widely in detail; for example, each of the evangelists may have followed a different Greek translation of Aramaic Matthew, and this would give rise to many minor divergencies. But, beyond that, there is the important factor that the evangelists are authors who wrote with a purpose in view and adapted the material to suit that purpose.

This last is an important point which will be considered more closely as we study each gospel. We find, for instance, that St. Luke, who writes Greek better than the others, is at pains to improve the style, and many of the lesser differences between his gospel and the others may be ascribed to that fact. On a wider reckoning we find that St. Matthew, who has written primarily for Jews, presumes that matters of Jewish interest will be readily understood. St. Luke, writing for Gentiles, consistently omits passages or references that are too specifically Jewish. We can see immediately that in this sphere differences between Matthew and Luke can be explained without difficulty.

It is hoped that the influence of one gospel on another will be more clearly understood when the individual gospels have been studied. But it is important, even at this stage, to have some notion of the relationship between them. We can see, dimly at least, how differences and apparent contradictions can be reasonably explained. Not everything will be clear, but it should be obvious that it is only by facing up honestly to undoubted difficulties that we can hope to understand the gospels. We should gratefully avail of the light won for us by the painstaking labors of sincere and dedicated scholars. To close one's eyes to light and truth is not praiseworthy in one who professes to be a follower of him who is Light and Truth.

III
The Cultural Milieu

1. Semitic Background

Except for St. Luke, the evangelists—and the other New Testament writers as well—were Jews; but even St. Luke is not really an exception because his gospel is still fundamentally Semitic. The Semitic flavor and background of the gospels is something we should strive to appreciate, for it is an essential part of the gospels and cannot be overlooked without danger of misinterpreting them. We must not measure them by our Western standards, but we should, rather, seek to understand the mentality of the evangelists, and this calls for a certain readjustment.

Our Western culture has its roots in that of Greece and Rome, and the Greek heritage, especially, has influenced our ways of thought. We spontaneously think and speculate by means of abstract ideas, and we commonly use abstract terms. This manner of thought comes naturally to us, and we imagine that all men think in precisely the same way. What we must realize is that the Semitic mind works differently, and Semitic outlook and culture are different from ours.

For us "to know" means to grasp an idea, but for the Semite it involves much more than that. "Knowledge" of God, in biblical language, is not a speculative notion of God, it includes the acceptance of all he stands for; it includes the service of God. The man who "knows" God is one who lives in the presence of God, one whose "knowledge" is a rule of conduct. For the Semite, God is not an abstract essence, a pure spirit—he is Creator, Judge, Father.

We are inclined to regard the Bible, including the gospels, as a sort of textbook (if not a book of texts); we seek there a set of doctrines and we are somewhat ill at ease because the teaching is not neatly arranged in logical order. What we should look for is the living image of a God who acts, who enters into our history, who speaks to our hearts. We conceive of God as a Pure Spirit; the Old Testament can speak of God as the shepherd of his people: "I myself will be the shepherd of my sheep" Ez. 34, 15—words that are echoed by the Son of God: "I am the good shepherd" John 10, 11.14. God can appear as the spouse of Israel: "Your Maker is your husband, the Lord of hosts is his name" Isa. 54, 5, and the New Testament teaches Christians to address him confidently as "Father." We have boiled down the doctrines of the faith, and set them out in precise, technical terms, and thrown them into the form of a catechism; but Jesus taught in parables. He took striking examples from everyday life and he spoke the language of poetry; and no matter how sublime the teaching, his words are always simple and concrete and full of imagery.

We are not, obviously, trying to disparage systematic theology, but it should be kept in mind that our theology, as a system, grew up later than the gospels. It has its roots in the Bible, in the New Testament especially, but it speaks another language; it translates the striking, sometimes daring, images of Semitic speech into precise, carefully framed formulas. In doing this it renders a very necessary service, but we should not expect to find the same scientific terminology in the Scriptures, no more than we ought to regard the Bible as a theological treatise. We lose the whole flavor of the gospel if we want to have its teaching parcelled out in neat categories. The gospels contain words of life, not only because they are a source of spiritual life, but also because they are living, fresh and vital.

In this scientific age we are plagued by a passion for

material exactitude, and this attitude is very well illustrated in the field of history. There have been some attempts to fit the ministry of our Lord into a detailed day by day chronology, but such attempts do violence to the texts and hinder the real understanding of the word of God. And if we turn to the Old Testament we find that its historians were, by our standards, rather casual. They were little worried by exact chronology and they quite regularly omitted facts that did not suit their point of view or their purpose. They have given us history that has glaring gaps and this shortcoming is, to our eyes, all the less excusable because they have often indicated that they had much more information at their disposal. So, judged by our standards, they were at fault—but may we legitimately measure them by modern standards? We can turn the argument right about and say that for Old Testament writers history in the modern style would be meaningless because it entirely misses the one thing that can give it meaning.

The Old Testament historian had God always in mind and saw the hand of God in everything that happened. In the light of this truth, this profound realization, details like exact chronology are seen in proper perspective. We pay lip service to the dogma of divine Providence, yet, in practice, we have lost sight of the constant activity of God in history. Does our more exact technique really compensate for the loss of that comforting vision?

All this applies in a special way to the gospels. Here we find not only the Providence of God but God Incarnate, a God who not only acts in history but has become a fact of history. The gospels are not catechisms in which we find doctrines of faith and morals neatly catalogued and expressed in precise theological terms. Instead we read of a Man who is the Son of God, who lived among us and taught and suffered and died and rose from the dead. He was born of the Jewish race, and came and preached to Jews in the concrete, picturesque language of Semites. And the evangelists, though they wrote in Greek, were faithful to the Semitic culture that was theirs and his. We should be grateful that this is so, for we have gained the poetry of the words of Jesus.

The least we might do is to make an effort to understand this mentality that is so different from ours. If we do no more than realize that the gospels were written nearly two thousand years ago and that they are a product of Semitic culture, we shall understand that here, too, there is room for misunderstanding. If we persist in treating them as twentieth century products of European thought, we cannot fail to do them violence.

At this point it might be well to reflect that the Semitic coloring of the gospels is in harmony with the composition of the primitive Church. The Church which Christ had come on earth to found was inaugurated at Pentecost when the Holy Spirit descended on those who were gathered together (Acts 2, 1-2), that is to say, the Apostles, with some women including Mary the mother of Jesus, and his brethren (1, 13-14). This means that, when it came into existence, the Church was composed exclusively of Jews, it was some little time before Gentile elements joined it. And this fact, together with the Jewish blood of Jesus and of the great Apostle of the Gentiles, surely more than balances the other fact that Christ was condemned to death by his own people. There is no basis in the gospels for anti-Semitism in any shape or form.

2. The Old Testament in the Gospels

The Semitic background does not concern only the mentality of the Apostles and evangelists, it extends, too, to the influence of the Old Testament on the gospels. When we realize what the Old Testament is, this influence is seen to be inevitable. The Israelites were the chosen People, raised up by God for a very special purpose: they were to bear witness to the true God, and prepare the way for the coming of his Messiah, the Anointed One whom he would send. The Old Testament is the history of the dealing of God with his people. We find, across a recurring cycle of infidelity, punishment, repentance and more unfaithfulness, a growth in doctrine and spirituality, a deepening religious sense which had its finest expression in the prophets. We see the plan of God being realized despite the shortcomings of men and in face of their malice. A marked and constant tendency of the Old Testament writers is that they look to the future, to the fulfilment of the saving plan of God.

The evangelists knew that the time of salvation had dawned, the Messiah had appeared among men. In the light of this manifestation they read the Old Testament with a new understanding. We should realize that the Apostles and disciples and evangelists knew their Bible thoroughly; even St. Luke, who was not a Jew, had studied it closely. In this they were faithful followers of their Master, for Christ made frequent use of Scripture in his teaching.

We may accept all this, and yet find ourselves at times—this has particular reference to St. Matthew—disconcerted by a vague and seemingly quite artificial reference to Scripture. Thus, when he has told us that the holy Family, on their return from Egypt, settled in Nazareth, the evangelist adds that this was "in order that what was spoken by the prophets might be fulfilled: 'He shall be called a Nazarene' " (2, 23). Significantly, the reference is to "the prophets" for the precise text is nowhere to be found. St. Matthew was evidently thinking of a *nazir*, one dedicated to God as in Judges 13, 5.7, and he read this into the word "Nazareth"; the Old Testament is full of similar word-play and popular etymology—it must be evaluated as such.

However, a superficial reference to Scripture is the exception and the evangelists' use of the Old Testament is particularly enlightened. They do not regard the prophets as sort of fortunetellers, and they do not seek to show an exact correspondence between prophecy and fulfilment. Nor do they try to demonstrate, as was attempted in later ages, that everything in the Old Law has direct reference to Christ. Closer study of their method has established that they concentrated on certain passages, mainly from Isaias, Jeremias, some of the minor prophets and Psalms, and the sections in question were considered as units and taken in their totality.

As a rule only a particular verse of one of these passages is quoted, but the whole context should be kept in mind if the true meaning of the citation is to be established. We see, for example, that Matthew and Mark place the first verse of Ps. 21 ("My God, my God, why have you forsaken me?") on the lips of Jesus on the Cross. St. John instead quotes v. 11 of the same psalm: "They divided my garments among them and for my clothing they cast lots." In each case it is not the isolated verse but the whole psalm that should be considered. And the psalm, opening on a note of dereliction, ends as a hymn of thanksgiving for deliverance (vv. 19-21), and so, admirably, fits the double aspect of the Passion of our Lord. The two passages that have most influenced the gospels are Isa. 53—the Servant of God—, and Dan. 7—the Son of Man. These will be dealt with at some length when we study the gospel of Mark.

The prophecies of the Old Testament are interpreted according to the evangelists' understanding of history, and the history of the people of God followed a plan designed by God. But the pattern into which the events of the Old Testament fall is not clearly seen until it is illuminated by the revealing light of the gospel. The Old is only a prelude to the New, but it is the same God who has brought to pass both the one and the other. And so the evangelists looked to the Old Testament to find the threads that ran through it, reaching to Christ.

So much we can see for ourselves but we have, besides, a guarantee that this interpretation of Scripture is not arbitrary but is divinely guided. St. Luke tells us that our Lord instructed the disciples on the road to Emmaus: "Beginning with Moses and going through all the prophets, he interpreted to them in all the Scriptures the things that concerned himself." 24, 27. And when the time came for him to leave his Apostles he addressed them for the last time: "These are my words which I spoke to you while I was still with you: everything written about me in the Law of Moses, the Prophets and the Psalms must be fulfilled. Then he opened their minds to understand the Scriptures." 24, 44-45. Thus enlightened, the apostolic Church discovered in the Old Testament the plan of God that found its fulfilment in Christ their Lord.

IV

Authorship of the First Gospel

1. Testimony of Tradition

The unanimous tradition of the early Church is that St. Matthew was the first of the four evangelists to write a gospel, and that he wrote it in Aramaic. That tradition is quite definite, as we shall see. However, the gospel of Matthew, as it has come to us in the New Testament, was written in Greek, and the relationship between the original Aramaic and the later Greek gospel raises a question that we shall have to consider.[1] But first we must establish and examine the tradition we speak of.

The earliest witness of tradition is that of Papias, who was bishop of Hierapolis in Phrygia (Asia Minor) about 130. He was the author of a five-volume work: *Explanation of the Lord's Sayings*. This work is not extant but some few passages of it have been preserved by the Church historian Eusebius. Papias got his information from "John the Elder"—who is not John the Apostle, as some have thought, though he was clearly a man of the first Christian generation, one who had known the Apostles. Thus Papias' testimony regarding the origin of Matthew is of great weight. Here is what he says: "Matthew, in Aramaic, grouped in order the sayings, and each translated them according to his ability."

It was long argued, in non-Catholic circles, that by sayings (in Greek *logia*) is meant a *collection* of sayings of our Lord, a work that was quite distinct from the gospel of Matthew. Many Catholics, on the other hand, have held that *logia* here is equivalent to "gospel." In fact both views are incorrect. *Logia* cannot mean "gospel," but neither does it, in the context, refer to a mere collection of sayings. When we compare this statement of Papias with his statement regarding Mark, the real meaning of the former is seen to be: "Matthew, in Aramaic, grouped in order (in his gospel) the sayings (of the Lord). . . ." The point at issue is that in Matthew the sayings of our Lord are, in fact, grouped in five long discourses, while in Mark there is no such order.

Other witnesses are:

Irenaeus (end of second century): "Matthew, in the language of the Hebrews, published a gospel when Peter and Paul were preaching in Rome and founding the Church there."

Eusebius (third century): "Matthew wrote a gospel in Hebrew i.e., Aramaic)." [2]

Origen (+ 254): "The first gospel was written in Aramaic for converted Jews by Matthew, who was a publican and an Apostle of Jesus Christ." We may thus summarize the verdict of early ecclesiastical tradition: Matthew the Apostle wrote a gospel in Aramaic for Jewish converts in Palestine.

2. The Greek Gospel

The tradition that St. Matthew was the author of an Aramaic gospel is unassailable. Since, as we have noted, it is not legitimate to limit the *logia,* mentioned by Papias, to a mere collection of sayings independent of this gospel, it follows that the Aramaic writing was a gospel in the strict sense and was, in fact, essentially a somewhat condensed form of the Palestinian catechesis, the original gospel plan drawn up by the Apostles. Papias tells us that it was soon translated into Greek ("each translated them according to his ability"), and it is one of these translations that is at the basis of our Greek Matthew—the gospel that we know.

Our gospel and the Aramaic gospel are substantially identical, but it does not follow that the Greek gospel is a direct translation of the other.[3] For one thing, the language of Matthew does not give one the impression that it is a translation; it has, for instance, a better Greek style than Mark, and the latter was certainly written in that language. However, this personal Greek style is not inconsistent with the tradition of the Aramaic origin of the gospel, for the source of Matthew is, most likely, not the Aramaic gospel itself, but a Greek translation of it. We have it on the testimony of Papias that not one only but many such Greek versions were made. The original gospel was meant for Jewish-Christians, but many of these, even in Palestine, were Greek-speaking, and they must have wanted versions in that language.

Besides, we have seen already that Matthew is dependent on other sources, notably on Mark and on a special source common to Matthew-Luke. Thus Matthew is, in the main, based on three accounts or documents: on a translation of Aramaic Matthew, on Mark, and on the source common to Matthew-Luke. All these are Greek sources. So Matthew, we say, is not in any way a direct translation from Aramaic writings. But, we insist, it is substantially identical with the original Aramaic gospel. Still, over and above that, it contains a number of additions.

It is quite certain that St. Matthew wrote the original Aramaic gospel, but it is not at all clear that it was he who wrote the Greek gospel, as we have it. The fact that we cannot be sure who wrote this is not as disturbing as might appear at first sight. We are quite certain, on the authority of the Church, which has accepted this gospel as Scripture, that the author of it was inspired—the fact that we are unable to name him is of secondary importance.

Of course, we shall continue to speak of the first gospel as the gospel according to St. Matthew. That is a convenient designation and, besides, the Apostle had a large part in its composition, even though it seems that it was not he who gave it its final form.

3. Destination and Date

Aramaic Matthew was obviously meant for Aramaic-speaking converts. It was essentially the Palestinian catechesis, and if we allow time for the development of the oral teaching we may put its composition at about 40-50. The Greek versions of it would date from more or less the same time.

Greek Matthew was addressed to Palestinian readers too, to Greek-speaking Jews and Jewish Christians. It is natural, then, that the Palestinian character of Matthew should be much more marked than that of the other Synoptics. And, indeed, we do find local color (Herod the *tetrarch*—his correct title 14, 1; the parasceve 27, 62), the use of traditional expressions (Raca, Gehenna 5, 22; Beelzebul 10, 25), allusions to Jewish customs (washing of hands before eating 15, 2; the wearing of phylacteries 23, 5)—and the author rarely feels it necessary to give an explanation of any of these. The gospel was written primarily for Jews, and this is something we should keep in mind when we read it.

Since Matthew is certainly dependent on Mark, to some extent, it cannot have been written before 64-65, which is the most likely date for Mark. Catholic writers have generally placed the composition of Matthew before 70, the date of the destruction of Jerusalem by the Romans. This event is foretold in Matt. 24, 15-20, and the text gives no hint (by filling out the details) that at the time of writing the prophecy had been fulfilled. But it may be that St. Matthew is here faithfully reproducing his sources and the passage may not necessarily be an argument for an early date.

So, in fact, we find eminent Catholic scholars—such as A. Wikenhauser[4]—who believe that our Greek Matthew was written shortly after 70. There is, then, some uncertainty, but it is clearly recognized today that the question of date is quite a secondary one since the gospels go back ultimately to the apostolic Church.

V

Literary Construction of the First Gospel

1. Plan of the Gospel[1]

A. Birth and Infancy of Christ, 1-2.

B.   I. The Promulgation of the Kingdom of Heaven, 3-7.
      a. Narrative Section, 3-4.
      b. Evangelical Discourse (Sermon on the Mount), 5-7.

  II. The Preaching of the Kingdom of Heaven, 8-10.
      a. Narrative Section (Ten Miracles), 8-9.
      b. Apostolical Discourse, 10.

  III. The Mystery of the Kingdom of Heaven, 11, 1-13, 52.
      a. Narrative Section, 11-12.
      b. Discourse: Seven Parables, 13, 1-52.

  IV. The Church, Firstfruits of the Kingdom of Heaven, 13, 53-18, 35.
      a. Narrative Section, 13, 53-17, 27.
      b. Ecclesiastical Discourse, 18.

  V. The Near Advent of the Kingdom of Heaven, 19-25.
      a. Narrative Section, 19-22 (+ Discourse, 23).
      b. Eschatological Discourse, 24-25.

C. Passion and Resurrection, 26-28.

If we leave aside the Infancy-narrative and the Passion-narrative, the central portion of the gospel of Matthew falls naturally into five parts, each containing a narrative and a discourse section. Each of the discourses has a brief introduction: 5, 1-2; 10, 1-5; 13, 1-3; 18, 1-2; 24, 1-3, and each is closed by a stereotyped formula: "And it came to pass, when Jesus had finished these sayings . . ." 7, 28; 11, 1; 13, 53; 19, 1; 26, 1.

Chapter 23, our Lord's severe censure of the Scribes and Pharisees, does not quite fit into this plan, for it is clear that Chs. 24-25 form the discourse which corresponds to the narrative section Chs. 19-22. It seems that Ch. 23 has been inserted into the original plan by the evangelist, and the fifth part is really built on the same model as the others.

The five central parts of Matthew are not so many disconnected units, there is a close link between them. The narrative indicates the progressive movement of events and the discourses illustrate a parallel progress in the Messianic concept of the Kingdom of heaven. Here is a summary of their content[2]—the numbers refer to the sections indicated in the plan:

After his baptism in Judea, which marked the inauguration of his public ministry as Messiah, our Lord began, in Galilee, to preach the coming of the Kingdom of heaven. In the Sermon on the Mount he laid down the conditions for participation in the Kingdom (I). He continued to propagate the Good News and he supported his teaching by working many miracles. His renown grew and crowds flocked to him. He chose his disciples, who became his constant companions, and he commissioned them to preach the Kingdom. To that end he instructed them and he pointed out particularly that they must be ready to face all dangers, even death (II). Christ himself encountered difficulties: the violent opposition of the Jewish authorities and the apathy of the crowd. Many of his parables were addressed to his opponents, who did not heed the clear warnings of these parables or listen to his appeals, but hardened their hearts against his message. The secret of the Kingdom—that it is present in his words and works—was revealed only to the few chosen and faithful ones (III).

At this stage Christ gave himself to the formation of his disciples—he knew that the time was short, the crisis was near. He still had compassion on the multitude, but he did not preach to them any more, and he likewise avoided discussion with the Jewish leaders. He organized the earthly phase of the Kingdom by instituting the Church with Peter as foundation. He instructed the Apostles in their duties to the community (IV). At last he left Galilee altogether. His going to Jerusalem was a journey to death. He censured the Jewish leaders in the presence of a crowd that was once again enthusiastic. His last discourse, the eschatological* prophecies, was for the Apostles alone (V).

The Infancy and Passion narratives are not extraneous to this plan but fit in to form one broader, unified plan. Indeed, the whole gospel has been characterized as "a drama in seven acts on the coming of the Kingdom of heaven."[4]

(i) The preparation: the Infant Messiah, 1-2.

(ii) The promulgation of the Program of the Kingdom in the Sermon on the Mount, 3-7.

(iii) The preaching of the Kingdom by specially instructed missionaries whose words were authenticated by the miracles of Christ, 8-10.

(iv) The opposition to the Kingdom—illustrated by the parables, 11, 1-13, 52.

(v) The beginnings in a group of disciples headed by Peter; these are the firstfruits of the Church whose way of life is sketched in the community discourse, 13, 53-18, 35.

(vi) The crisis which must precede the final appearance of the Kingdom—the eschatological discourse, 19-25.

(vii) The advent of the Kingdom in suffering and triumph through the Passion and Resurrection, 26-28.

2. The Discourses

St. Matthew presents the five great discourses of his gospel as discourses of our Lord, but we must correctly understand his method and realize his intention, for this arrangement is artificial and he was well aware of it. When we examine the discourses we find that each of them has been formed by grouping together related sayings of our Lord. In other words, these discourses contain teaching of Chirst that was given on various occasions and it is the evangelist who has formed this varied teaching into a unified "sermon."

The Sermon on the Mount (5-7) affords a good example of this method.[5] Our Lord formulated the special character, the new spirit of the Kingdom of God, in a discourse which Mark has omitted and which Matthew and Luke (6, 20-49) have preserved in widely different versions. The discourse in Matthew is much longer than that in Luke, but, on the other hand, many of the passages found in Matt. 5-7 are found elsewhere in Luke, in chapters 11, 13, 14 and 16. It can be shown that St. Luke has omitted, as being of little interest to his Gentile readers, all that concerned Jewish law and custom (Matt. 5, 17-6, 18). In general we may say that St. Matthew has added to the original Sermon and St. Luke has omitted some of it.

If the additions that St. Matthew has made to his source can be recognized and isolated we may get back to the original plan of the Sermon. The analysis that follows is in no way arbitrary but is based on a close and detailed study of the text of Matthew; however, within the scope of this work we must be satisfied with the result of that investigation.

In the first place it is necessary to show that St. Matthew has made additions, but this fact can be established without much difficulty; a study of the Lord's Prayer, for example, bears it out. St. Luke informs us that it was the sight of our Lord in prayer, alone, in an unspecified place, that moved his disciples to ask him to teach them to pray (11, 1), and in this the evangelist has undoubtedly given us the circumstances in which the Savior spoke the prayer. St Matthew, on the other hand, has presented the Our Father in the context of the Sermon on the Mount; it is not hard to understand why he has done so.

In Matt. 6, 1-18 we find, first, in v. 1, a general statement on the performance of good works. This is followed by a consideration of the three great Jewish works of piety: almsgiving, prayer and fasting. It can be seen that vv. 2-4, 5-6 and 16-18 treat each of these in exactly the same manner: a warning not to imitate the hypocrites is followed by an

indication of the proper attitude of disciples.[6] Now, this
uniform plan is disturbed by vv. 7-15.

What has happened is that St. Matthew has taken advantage of the reference to prayer, first to add a warning
against praying like the Gentiles (vv. 7-8) and then to give
the example of the perfect prayer (vv. 9-15). He even
carries the process a step further and in vv. 14-15 he de-
velops the idea, expressed in the Our Father (v. 12) on
forgiving others. So, in fact, we are given a summary of
our Lord's teaching on prayer.

When these and similar additions are recognized and
taken into account it would seem that the Sermon on the
Mount as St. Matthew knew it, that is to say before he
made the insertions, was along these lines:

Part I: Perfect justice

    General statement: Perfect justice (5, 17-20).

    Five concrete examples: (5, 21-24. 27-28. 33-37.
       38-42. 43-48).

Part II: Good works

    General statement (6, 1).

    Three concrete examples (6, 2-4. 5-6. 16-18).

Part III: Three warnings

    (a) Do not judge (7, 1-2)

       Example: Parable of the mote and the beam (3-5).

    (b) Beware of false prophets (7, 15)

       Example: Parable of the tree and its fruit (16-20).

    (c) Practice justice (7, 21)

       Example: Parable of the two houses (24-27).

The procedure of the discourse is uniform throughout:
a general recommendation is illustrated by concrete examples. The first recommendation (5, 20) is the most
general and it has five applications. The three sayings of
Ch. 7 refer directly to conduct—one example is enough to
illustrate each of them. The discourse is by no means a
mere collection of sayings but has a very real unity and is
highly original.

The many additions of St. Matthew have not changed the
plan of the discourse and the structure of the original is
preserved. But into this framework he has inserted material

taken from another source, one used by St. Luke also—
because almost all these sayings are found in Luke too,
though not as part of the Sermon. The passages in question
are numerous: Matt. 5, 13-16. 18-19. 25-26; 29-32. 36; 6,
7-15. 19-34; 7, 6-14. 22-23—in all about half of the discourse as St. Matthew presents it. These additions respond
to a desire for *completeness*. St. Matthew is manifestly anxious to give a view as wide as possible of the teaching of his
Master and to hold out the ideal of the perfect life to which
he had called his disciples. It is in the same spirit that he
has composed the other four discourses.

In Chapters 5-7 he is preoccupied with the conduct of
Christians and he tries to indicate all that the Master re-
quires of them. So he speaks of the duty of concord among
brethren (5, 25-26), and of forgiveness (6, 14-15). He
insists on detachment (6, 19-34) and on the necessity of
good works (7, 22-23). In short, he is concerned with
immediate results and he sees the Sermon on the Mount
as, primarily, a program of life, and that is why he fits in so
many sayings of Christ that have a bearing on conduct.
But these *are* our Lord's sayings, and we must never lose
sight of the fact that though the arrangement of these
chapters is the work of St. Matthew, the words are, all of
them, the words of Christ.

This whole question is not just a matter of literary
criticism, but has a practical bearing, for, if it can be shown
that isolated sayings of our Lord have been grouped together, that fact must be kept in mind in interpreting these
sayings. The context in which they are found, and their
relation to on another, are, in some degree at least, artificial.
It would be misleading, for instance, to take the Sermon
in Matt. 5-7 as one closely-knit unit, and study it as one
would a theological essay. There is a certain unity, and there
is a plan, but these chapters are, to a large extent, made
up of pre-existing and distinct parts. The realization of this
factor can save us from being disturbed by a lack of strict
logical order, and can prevent us from doing violence to the
text by reading into it a too rigid sequence of ideas.

St. Luke's approach to the Sermon is different from that
of St. Matthew, and it does not concern us here. But we

should like to note that Dom Dupont concludes his study of the method of both evangelists in terms that give further force to a point we were at pains to emphasize in an earlier chapter.

"These retouches indicate the concept which the evangelists had of their task and the preoccupations which guided them in their work. Their role, as they saw it, was not that of simple annalists. As evangelists they were very conscious of the concrete aspect of the teaching which they handed on and which was destined to nourish the Christian life of those for whom they wrote. They seem to have been more interested in the application of principles to conduct than in the principles as such. It was not enough for them to tell their readers what the Master had taught, they wanted to bring that teaching to bear on their lives. The spirit which animated their work was the spirit of the primitive Church. The gospel tradition is not to be conceived as a mechanically exact repetition of the words of Jesus; it is a question of witness, of testimony. The words of Jesus are living, life-giving words; the early Church passed them on clothed also with its own life." [7]

3. The Narratives

Distinct from the discourses, in literary style, are the narrative sections, which deal with the activity of our Lord, his journeys and miracles. Matthew, as we have seen, is later than Mark and has used that gospel, but it is also largely independent of Mark. This can be observed in the style of Matthew which is more polished that that of the second gospel. There are many Aramaisms[8] but these are not so frequent as in Mark. Yet, in the narratives, there is a large field of agreement between the two gospels. It is true that Mark has, generally, many vivid details not found in Matthew, but the latter may have deliberately employed a more austere style. If we take, for example, the account of the cure of Peter's mother-in-law (Matt. 8, 14-15; Mark 1, 29-31; Luke 4, 38-39) we find that the suppression of all accessory details in Matthew gives a certain solemnity to the narrative. At the same time Matthew also tends to be clearer than the others.

It is particularly in the narrative sections, too, that Matthew approaches most closely to the primitive catechesis of the apostolic Church. This, as we have seen, was first set down in the Aramaic gospel. It follows that when Matthew has less detail than Mark, this is not, or at least not always, because he has deliberately abbreviated Mark, but because he has gone beyond Mark and found the narrative in a simpler form (in the Aramaic gospel).

Matthew quickly became the most widely known and used of the gospels. By itself it forms the basis of ordinary Christian teaching on the life and doctrine of Chirst. That is why Father Lagrange can write:° "It is the first gospel that has always been dearest to pious souls and to preachers. St. Dominic included it and the Epistles of St. Paul among the few belongings he carried with him on his missionary journeys. The Christ of St. Matthew is less homely than the Christ of St. Mark who is so indulgent towards disciples slow to understand. He is less the Savior of the world than in Luke, and he is never called the Word as in John. He is the revealer of a doctrine that is essentially interior, and he is the founder of the Christian institution built on Peter. Meek and humble of heart, he does not quench the smoldering wick, but he challenges the hypocrites and unmasks them. He is the Messiah, a Lawgiver, not like Moses in the name of another, but as God: the only Son of God whom Israel had rejected but whom the Church has received. If St. Matthew, in his narrative, has not the striking realism of St. Mark, or the gentle charm of St. Luke; if his gaze is not fixed on divine things like that of St. John, he has many more sayings of Christ, sayings simple and straightforward, sayings that are so penetrating that one seems to hear them, with the accent and intonation almost, that they had on his lips. Indeed, the oldest witness of the Church's tradition, Papias, has seen in Matthew, above all else, *the divine Words*. It is these words, too, that we must study."

VI

Theological Ideas of the First Gospel

1. The Messiah

The first gospel is dominated by this idea: Jesus is the Messiah who was foretold and promised in the Old Testament and whose arrival was awaited by the Jews; but when he came his own people rejected him.

That our Lord is indeed the promised Messiah is proved first of all by reference to the prophets, and no other evangelist uses and cites the Old Testament so freely. In this respect the so-called "reflection-citations" (because they are personal "reflections" of the evangelist) are noteworthy. In them St. Matthew shows that Christ has fulfilled the Old Testament prophecies. There are ten such distinctive quotations:

Four in the Infancy-narrative: 1, 22-23; 2, 15. 17-18. 23.

Five in the central part of the gospel: 4, 14-16; 8, 17; 12, 17-21; 13, 35; 21, 4-5.

One in the Passion-narrative: 27, 9-10.

We may remark with regard to all of these:

(i) They are proper to Matthew. Neither the citations nor their introductory formulas are found elsewhere in the Synoptics, or in the New Testament for that matter.

(ii) All ten are personal reflections of the evangelist; all other quotations are attributed to our Lord or to some other character in the gospels.

(iii) The introductory formula is essentially the same in all ten citations: "In order that the oracle of (the Lord . . . Jeremias . . . the prophet) might be fulfilled" or "Then was fulfilled the oracle of (the Lord . . . Jeremias . . . the prophet)."

(iv) There is sometimes a certain artificiality in the application of these texts to events in the life of our Lord. (Cf. above: The Old Testament in the Gospels.) The quotations are easily detached from their context—this is because they have been added by the evangelist.

It would seem to follow that St. Matthew has been referring to a special collection of Old Testament "prooftexts," that is to say, to a list of Old Testament texts which were used by Christians as arguments to show that Christ had fulfilled the prophecies. This does serve to emphasize his purpose, but it is not only by means of Old Testament quotations that our Lord is shown to be the Messiah; the whole presentation of Matthew emphasizes the point.

Jesus the Messiah, as the evangelist saw him, was in a special way, the "son of David." The gospel begins with a genealogy which demonstrates that he was descended from David 1, 1. In fulfilment of the prophecy of Micheas (5, 1) he was born in David's city of Bethlehem 2, 5. As son of David he was "king of the Jews" and it was as such that his life was sought by Herod 2, 13-23. The Baptist's query 11, 2-3 does, despite appearances, receive a direct answer 11, 4-6, for the works there listed are the works of the Messiah (cf. Isa. 26, 19; 29, 18 f; 35, 5 f; 61, 1) and John must have concluded that he who did these things was indeed the Messiah. The healing of a man who had a blind and dumb spirit moved the people to ask if this were the son of David 12, 23. The two blind men 9, 27 and the pagan woman 15, 23 addressed him as "son of David." On his entry into Jerusalem this son of David was acclaimed by the people 21, 10 and received the homage of the children 21, 15.

Christ is, therefore, the promised King of Israel—but his own people rejected him. Before Pilate they fiercely called for his crucifixion, and thus, paradoxically, ensured the success of his mission. The open enmity of the Pharisees and leaders of the people is clear right through the gospels, but Matthew emphasizes the rejection of Christ by his own people. This is forcibly brought home in an episode of the Passion-narrative proper to Matthew: Pilate disclaimed responsibility by washing his hands, and *"the whole people cried out: His blood be upon us and upon our children"* 27, 24-25—it was the formal apostasy of the chosen people. This is the great tragedy that was so deeply to affect Paul, the passionate lover of his people (Rom 11).

2. Our Lord's Attitude to the Old law and to Jewish Teaching and Practice

St. Matthew stresses, much more than the other evangelists, the attitude of our Lord towards the Old Law. This is clearest in the Sermon on the Mount where Christ, the new Lawgiver, proclaims his law for the new people of God. But this does not mark a break with the Old Law: Christ came not to abolish the Law but to perfect it 5, 17. The Old Law, as it was interpreted by him and incorporated into his law, still remains in force. Not only that, but it has been brought to perfection by the setting up of love, love even of one's enemy, as the fulfilment of God's will 5, 44.

The six so-called "antitheses"—because they contrast the obligations of the Law with the far-reaching demands of Christ[1]—5, 21-48, show how the fulfilling of the Law is to be understood. These end with the recommendation: "Be you perfect as your heavenly Father is perfect" 5, 48. God in his mercy, justice and infinite goodness is to be the model for all human morality. This is no destruction of the Old Law, but is a mighty deepening of its true significance.

In much the same way St. Matthew is careful to show that Christ, in condemning the Pharisees, did not condemn the good points in their teaching 23, 3. We find that almsgiving, prayer and fasting—the chief Jewish acts of piety—are to be practiced by his disciples also, but without ostentation 6, 1-6. 16-18. And when the scribes and

Pharisees pass on the traditional doctrine received from Moses they speak with authority and should be followed without question 23, 2-3, even though their own practice is not to be imitated and their personal interpretations of the Law are not binding 23, 3.

The Jewish outlook was exclusive, nationalistic—contact with the Gentiles was avoided wherever possible—and it may be disconcerting to find that, on occasion, our Lord appeared to subscribe to this view. We find him forbidding his disciples to preach to the Samaritans and pagans 10, 5 and he himself declared that he was sent only to "the lost sheep of the house of Israel" 15, 24. But these passages must be seen in the context of the whole gospel. As the chosen people, the people of the divine promises, Israel had the right to hear the Good News *first*, it must first be evangelized—this is the meaning of 10, 5. Elsewhere it is clear that the Good News is for all. In the parable of the Wicked Husbandmen we are told that the Kingdom will be taken from Israel and given to a people that will produce its fruits 21, 43 (cf. 8, 11 f), and the gospel closes with the command to teach all nations 28, 19. The outlook is not narrow and racial but universalist.

It is interesting to note that St. Paul, whenever he came to any place where Jews were established, always preached first to them before he turned to the pagans. In this he was, as in all things, faithful to the teaching and practice of his Master.

3. The Kingdom of Heaven

(1) THE KINGDOM OF GOD

Christ, the son of David, the Messiah, came to found a Kingdom, and in his presentation of the preaching of Jesus St. Matthew insists on the theme of the Kingdom of heaven. The reader of the gospels will, no doubt, have noted that Mark and Luke speak, not of the "kingdom of heaven" but of the "kingdom of God" and it may seem to him that there is a corresponding difference in meaning. But this is not so. In Matthew's phrase "heaven" is used because the Jews, particularly about the time of our Lord, avoided, whenever possible, using the divine name (in much the same way we avoid using the name "Jesus"). So, "kingdom of heaven" is exactly the same as "kingdom of God." It is, indeed, very likely that our Lord, addressing Jews, employed the current expression and spoke of the "kingdom of heaven."

The basic idea of the "Kingdom of God" is that of the "rule" or "reign" of God. This corresponds to the meaning of the Aramaic *malkutha* (the term used by our Lord): "kingship," "kingly rule," "sovereignty." But while the reign of God is the primary idea, that of domain or kingdom is also necessarily implied; there can be no reign, in any real sense, without a kingdom.

Our Lord, in speaking of the Kingdom of God, quite obviously took it for granted that his hearers would know what he meant. He spoke of something already familiar to them and he did not have to begin by explaining the term. In the Old Testament, however, the expression occurs only rarely and then in the later books (e.g., Tob. 13, 1; Ps. 145, 11-12; Dan. 3, 100; Wisd. 10, 10). But in non-biblical Jewish literature there was frequent reference to the Kingdom of God. This was largely due to the tendency, already noted, to avoid mention of the name of God or to speak of him in abstract terms. For instance, in Isa. 24, 23, instead of "Yahweh² shall reign" the Aramaic version reads: "the Kingdom of God will be manifest." Yet, though the name is not prevalent, the reality of the Kingdom of God is very much in evidence in the Old Testament and the Synoptic use of the term has Old Testament roots. (E.g., Num. 23, 21; 1 Sam. 12, 13; Isa. 52, 7; 1 Chr. 29, 11.)

In the teaching of our Lord the Kingdom is, first and foremost, an intervention of God in history. That is true also of the Old Testament concept, but in the New Testament view the divine intervention is made manifest in the coming of the Son of God. God intervenes in history—in other words, it is he who establishes his Kingdom, it is his work. He is like the sower, like the owner of the vineyard, like the king who gave a feast. And he, too, grants vitality to the Kingdom so that it grows, from within, like a seed, so that it spreads out, irresistibly, as leaven permeates the mass of dough. But though it is the work of God, yet, ultimately and in the concrete, the Kingdom is identified with the work and with the very person of Jesus Christ.

This insistence on the supernatural origin of the Kingdom and on its spiritual nature does not mean that the idea of a domain can be ignored. God, in establishing his reign among men, sets up a Kingdom in which he will be acknowledged as King, and over which he will reign. That is why there is question of entering into the Kingdom (Matt. 5, 20; 7, 21; 18, 3). That is why it is like a feast in which those who belong to the Kingdom have a place (8, 11). In the interpretation of the parable of the Cockle we read that the Son of Man will send his angels who will "gather out of his kingdom all scandals and all evil-doers" Matt. 13, 41. In these and similar passages it is clear that a kingdom is meant and not a reign only.

The question may be asked whether, in the teaching of our Lord, this Kingdom is already present, or whether he sees it as something lying wholly in the future. The truth of the matter is that he considered it under both aspects, for it has this two-fold aspect. In many passages of the gospels it appears as a future reality (cf. Matt. 10, 7; 24, 14) and many of the parables refer to a kingdom that awaits its completion and perfection: the mustard-seed, the Wheat and the Cockle (13, 24-32. 47-50). But these same parables just as obviously presuppose that the foundation of the Kingdom has already been laid and indicate a slow but sure development—the mustard-seed grows and the sown wheat ripens to the harvest.

This growth is the gift of God and in the final phase, at the moment of completion and perfection, God himself will intervene in a special way. But at the same time, the divine intervention in history is already present in the coming of Christ. That "time" (the Messianic age) of which the prophets spoke is here, and Jesus can reproach his contemporaries with failing to recognize the signs of the times (16, 3). The Apostles contemplate that which the prophets and just men of the Old Law had desired to see but had not seen (13, 16). True, the full realization still lies in the future, but nonetheless, the Kingdom has been quietly introduced into the "midst of" the Jews (Luke 17, 20-21) and the hearers of Jesus are summoned to take sides for or against it. In short, we may say that with the coming of Christ the Kingdom made its appearance on earth, but this Kingdom will reach its full development only in heaven.

(2) THE CHURCH—THE KINGDOM OF GOD ON EARTH[8]

Jesus regarded himself as the Messiah and, in the Old Testament and Jewish perspective, there could be no Messiah without a Messianic community. He called himself a shepherd, in the sense of Ezech. 34—there is no shepherd without a flock. He called himself Son of Man, with reference to the book of *Daniel*, and the Son of Man of *Daniel*, while he is the future heavenly king, is also the representative of the Messianic people, the Saints of the Most High (Dan. 7, 13-14. 27).

It follows that the idea of a Church is demanded by the idea of Messiah. The essential connection between them is clearer still in the idea of Messiah as our Lord conceived it, and this is brought out in his teaching on the Kingdom of God. The intervention of God, foretold by the prophets, took the form of the founding, on earth, of a Kingdom, for, though the Reign of God had come in the person of Christ, that Reign had to find concrete expression in the world, it had to find its repercussions among men. The Church has its role to play in the full actualization of the Kingdom; yet the Church, on earth, is not final, it is not an end in itself—it looks to the consummation of the Kingdom of God in heaven.

If the Church is so linked to the whole purpose and to the person of Christ, it follows that he did not found it by any one word or by any one act—it is the result of his whole saving action. Still, there are three episodes which mark three of the essential stages in its foundation: Christ's choice of the Twelve, his promise to Peter at Caesarea Philippi (with the completion of each episode after the Resurrection), and his Last Supper. These are the decisive moments in the emergence of the Church; after Easter, and especially at Pentecost, it had passed the embryonic stage and became a reality among men.

A. *The Twelve*

From among his disciples Jesus chose a special group as his collaborators, and both the number of the Twelve and their function are meaningful. The (symbolic) importance of the number is demonstrated by the preoccupation of the Christian community to replace Judas and restore the full number (Acts 1, 15-26). It is so sacrosanct that Paul speaks of an apparition of the Risen Christ to the Twelve (1 Cor. 15, 5) when in reality there were only eleven Apostles. The number is manifestly symbolical and has an obvious relation to the twelve tribes of Israel. Christ came to establish the new people of God and he gathered around him the "little flock" (Luke 12, 32) which would be the nucleus of a new society. The number twelve is a reminder of the twelve tribes of the first people of God; the new people will be a continuation of the old, in a more perfect form, and the unity of the divine plan is emphasized.

The prophetical theme of the "Remnant" has its place here too. Faced with the successive infidelities of the chosen people, and the inevitable punishment that followed, the prophets foretold that the divine justice would preserve a "Remnant," which, purified by God, would inherit the Messianic Kingdom. It is a favorite theme of Isaias (6, 13; 10, 20-22; 17, 4-6 . . .). In the eyes of Ezechiel—and this is really the idea of Isaias too, though not so explicitly—the Remnant is not merely the debris of something that has passed away—a brand snatched from the burning—it is a seed.

For the essential fact about the Remnant is not its smallness, but the interior transformation which is wrought in it by the action of Yahweh. In this perspective the Remnant of which the prophets spoke is the community of those who, having put their faith in Yahweh, will be transformed by him, and built up into something new. In the very same way Jesus wished to gather around him a group of faithful disciples who would be the foundation of a new people of God, a new Israel, the Messianic Kingdom.

This process of choice and transformation can be traced in the gospels. As enthusiasm towards our Lord waned and opposition to his message grew, the Twelve came more and more to play the role of the Remnant in the prophetical sense. "Under the purifying and saving action of Christ they became the 'little flock' gathered in from an Israel doomed to destruction because of its lack of faith. They are the few who were chosen when the many who had been called did not accept the invitation and were excluded from the Kingdom of God (Matt. 22, 14)."⁴

Our Lord had a double purpose in view in choosing his Apostles, as we gather from Mark 3, 14. First he wanted them "to be with him" in order to form them and fill them with his spirit. But his principal purpose was to make them associates in the founding of the Kingdom of God on earth. In order to prepare them for this task he sent them to preach, to drive out devils and to heal the sick (Matt. 10, 1). He sent them out just as the Father had sent him (10, 5-40). In the eyes of men they were representatives of Jesus, and, as it were, extensions of his person: whoever received them received him; whoever despised them despised him (10, 40).

But as long as Jesus was still on earth there could be no question of personal initiative for them. They were instituted in view of the future and it was only after the Resurrection that the Twelve were given full powers: the commission to recruit disciples from all peoples, the power to baptize and to forgive sins (28, 18-20). But even then they still remain the representatives of Christ, for he will be always with them (28, 20) and they will act in his name under the direction of the Spirit he had promised to send upon them (Luke 24, 49).

B. *The Promise to Peter*

The promise made to Peter at Caesarea Philippi (Matt. 16, 13-19) took place at a turning point in the ministry of Christ. The people, though impressed by his miracles, had shown that they understood nothing of the mystery of his person. But what of his privileged disciples? He now turned to them: "Who do *you* say that I am?" (16, 15) And in the name of the Twelve Peter acknowledged the Messianic dignity of Jesus. By that fact, and in that moment, the little group drew apart from the unbelieving Jews and stood revealed as the Remnant foretold by the prophets—not just the few surviviors left after a catastrophe, but the seed of a new growth. And so our Lord went on to announce the foundation of his Church with Peter as its foundation stone (16, 17-19).

The passage Matt. 16, 13-19 should be seen against the background of Dan. Ch. 7. Just as in *Daniel* the triumph of the Son of Man, who includes in some fashion in his person the Saints of the Most High (the Messianic community), follows on the destruction of the pagan empires, so in Matthew a new community is set up and receives the promise of victory over the kingdom of death. This city (*Sheol,* the Old Testament place of the sojourn of the dead, the "city of death"—and not "hell" in our sense) is regarded as one whose gates, hitherto firmly closed, will be forced by Christ the conqueror of death, and by the Church which continues his saving work. It is in this active sense, and not in the sense of a mere passive resistance that the "shall not prevail" should be understood. "The gates of death cannot resist the works of salvation; despite the efforts of Satan they must yield up those whom they have swallowed." [5]

Peter is not only the foundation of the new community, but to him has been given the faculty of "binding" and of "loosing," that is to say, of admitting into the Messianic Kingdom, or of excluding from that Kingdom and also of making decisions in doctrinal and moral matters.

"Just like the City of Death, the City of God has gates, gates which open only to those who are worthy. Peter receives their keys. It is his office to open or to bar, in the Church, the way to the Kingdom of heaven. 'To bind' or 'to loose' were technical terms in the language of the Jewish rabbis. First of all they indicated excommunication —to which one was condemned (bound) or from which one was absolved (loosed). Their meaning was extended to the doctrinal and juridical decisions in the sense of forbidding (binding) or permitting (loosing). Peter, as major-domo—the keys are the insignia of this office, cf. Isa. 22, 22—of the House of God, will exercise the disciplinary power of admitting or excluding as he sees fit, and he will also regulate the life of the community by opportune decisions in doctrinal and moral matters. His sentences and decrees will be ratified by God in heaven." [6]

3. THE LAST SUPPER AND THE NEW ALLIANCE

We regard the Last Supper only as the occasion on which our Lord instituted the sacrament of the Eucharist, and we tend to forget that by that very fact, and because of the circumstances that surrounded the event, he established a new Covenant, a new Alliance between God and the new people of God. St. Luke (22, 15) quite explicitly states that the Last Supper was a Paschal meal, and this is at least strongly suggested in Matt. 26, 17-19. Since Christ came not to abolish the Law but to fulfil it (Matt. 5, 17), so now he set about "fulfilling" the Jewish Pasch (Luke 22, 16) by instituting a new and better Pasch. The Jewish rite was transformed into one incomparably higher.

But there is more to it than that. The full significance of the words of our Lord at the Last Supper, and the circumstances of the occasion, have, because of apologetical preoccupations—the anxiety to defend the Catholic doctrine of the Eucharist—been overlooked. Yet, when he declared: "This is my blood (the blood), of the covenant" Matt. 26, 28, he must have had in mind the words of Moses at the conclusion of the covenant at Sinai: "This is the blood of the covenant which Yahweh has made with you" Ex. 24, 8 and he was conscious that he was, at that moment, replacing the economy of Moses. In speaking of the new Alliance he must have recalled the great oracle of Jer. 31, 31-34 (which has an important place in the New Testament):

> "Behold the days are coming, says Yahweh, when I will make a new covenant with the house of Israel and the house of Juda, not like the covenant which I made with their fathers on the day when I took them by the hand to bring them out of the house of Egypt—my covenant which they broke! . . . But this is the covenant which I will make with the house of Israel after those days, says Yahweh: I will plant my law deep within them and I will write it upon their hearts.

Then I will be their God and they shall be my people. And no longer shall they need to teach one another: 'Learn to know Yahweh,' for they shall all know me, from the least of them to the greatest; for I will forgive their iniquity and I will remember their sin no more." (Cf. II Cor. 3, 6; Rom. 11, 27; Heb. 8, 6-13; 9, 15 ff; 1 John 5, 20.)

The very mention of a *new* Alliance marks a link with the Old. But though it had been prepared by the mysterious events and rites of the Old Testament, it was still something fresh and original, it pointed to a new beginning. And it was the little band of Twelve, confirmed by the promise made to Peter, which became the firstfruits of the new Alliance that God had made with men, an Alliance sealed by the blood of the Son of God.

So it was that the new people of God, the Church, came into being, and the Kingdom of God was firmly established on earth.

4. The Son of God

In Matthew, and the other two Synoptics, our Lord is frequently called "Son of God." We must realize that this designation is not quite so obvious as it appears and we would do well to examine it more closely. For the biblical title, "Son of God" does not necessarily imply natural divine sonship. It can, and very often does, indicate an adoptive sonship which follows on the divine choice and establishes particularly intimate relations between God and his creatures.

In the Old Testament the term is applied to angels (Job 1, 6; 38, 7; Ps. 28, 1), to the chosen people (Ex. 4, 22; Wisd. 18, 13), to the Israelites (Deut. 14, 1; Osee 2, 1), to their leaders (Ps. 82, 6), to the king (II Sam. 7, 14; Ps. 89, 27). In later Judaism, with the advent of individualistic religion (that is, of a more personal relationship between the individual and God, because formerly the Israelite had regarded himself only as one of a community—the chosen people) the pious man became a "son of God" (Ecclus. 4, 10; 23, 1; Wisd. 2, 16). In Jewish literature the Messiah was not called son of God—which is understandable in view of the very wide meaning of the title. So it seems that at the time of our Lord "Son of God" had no necessary Messianic connotation.

In the Synoptic gospels the title "Son of God" is often colored by the evangelists' faith in the true divine Sonship of Christ. We can see this influence in Matt. 16, 16—where Peter acknowledges the Messiahship of Jesus—when we compare this text with Mark 8, 29.[7] It is very clear too in Matt. 14, 33 (cf. Mark 6, 51 f). We must not suppose that the title had originally the full meaning in the mouth of Satan (Matt. 4, 3-6), or the demoniacs (8, 29). The declaration of the centurion at the foot of the Cross is a striking case in point. According to Mark he says: "Truly this man was a son of God" 15, 39, whereas Luke has: "Certainly this man was innocent" 23, 47. This title even at the Baptism (Matt. 3, 17) and at the Transfiguration (17, 5) did not, for its hearers, imply more than the special divine favor bestowed on the Messiah. However, it would seem that the solemn question of the high priest (Matt. 26, 63) did extend to the superhuman rank which Jesus claimed.

For the title, "Son of God" is, of course, open to the meaning of true divine Sonship. In fact Christ did suggest this by designating himself as "Son" (Matt. 17, 26-27; 21, 37). In Matt. 7, 21 he calls God "my Father." So, too, he never speaks of "our Father" (except in the prayer which is meant for his disciples) but always of "my Father" or "your Father." The most explicit text of all, which is quite like the style of St. John, but certainly belongs to the Synoptic tradition, clearly asserts his divine Sonship: "All things have been delivered to me by my Father, and no one knows the Son except the Father, as no one knows the Father except the Son and he to whom the Son chooses to reveal him." Matt. 11, 27. These statements, confirmed by the Resurrection, give to the title "Son of God" the properly divine meaning which it has, for example, in St. Paul.

Yet we must realize that during the lifetime of Jesus the disciples were not conscious of the full implication of his claims; the gospels make no secret of the fact that they did not understand him. Certain texts of St. John are apposite here. After the cleansing of the Temple, and again after the entry into Jerusalem on Palm Sunday, the evangelist remarks that the disciples did not grasp the full meaning of these events until after the Resurrection, 2, 22; 12, 16. (Cf. also 13, 7; Luke 9, 45; 18, 34.) Similarly, our Lord had, not once but many times, foretold his death and resurrection, and yet when Peter and the beloved disciple came to the empty tomb we are faced with the blunt statement: "for as yet they did not know the scripture, that he must rise from the dead" 20, 9. They had not yet received the Holy Spirit, and it was he alone who would help them to understand the teaching of Christ 14, 26; 16, 13.

But when they did receive the Paraclete, that faith that was theirs after the Resurrection, and especially after Pentecost, was based on the words of their Master, for he had indeed claimed to be, in the strictest sense, the Son of God. It is by men filled with this faith, and certain of this great truth, that the gospels were written; but this fuller perception was not found during the lifetime of our Lord.

We shall consider the divine claims of Christ once again when we come to St. Mark and there we shall see that, paradoxically, the title "Son of Man" is more significant than the title "Son of God."

VII

Authorship of the Second Gospel

1. Testimony of Tradition

The tradition of the early Church is quite unanimous in attributing the second gospel to St. Mark. As in the case of Matthew the most important witness is that of Papias:

> And the Elder said this also: "Mark, having become the interpreter of Peter, wrote down accurately all that he remembered of the things said and done by the Lord, but not however in order." For neither did he hear the Lord, nor did he follow him, but afterward, as I said, (followed) Peter who adapted his teaching to the needs (of his hearers), but not as though he were drawing up a connected account of the Lord's sayings. So then Mark made no mistake in thus recording some things just as he remembered them, for he took care to omit nothing that he heard and to make no false statement.

The Elder's[1] statement ends with the first sentence, the rest being the opinion of Papias himself. This second part is really a commentary on the statement of the Elder.[2] The statement and the comment each contain three parts:

(i) The Elder remarks that St. Mark is the interpreter of Peter.

(ii) He then notes the essential quality of his work: St. Mark has written accurately all his recollections of the words of Peter.

(iii) He concludes by saying that St. Mark did not put in order the sayings of Christ.

These three points are taken up by Papias, but in a different order:

(i) He explains the dependence of St. Mark: he is not a disciple of the Lord, but at a later date became a disciple of Peter.

(ii) Then he takes the third point of the Elder—the order of Mark. He remarks on the homely method of Peter who did not try to make an ordered grouping of the sayings, and St. Mark, his faithful disciple, proceeded in the same fashion.

(iii) Papias defends the accuracy of Mark's account; he had only one purpose: to omit nothing of what he had heard and to add nothing that was inaccurate.

Thus Papias not only unhesitatingly attributes the gospel to St. Mark, but goes out of his way to defend the evangelist's method. He appears to be replying to unfavorable criticism of the ordering of material in Mark as compared with that of Matthew.

Other witnesses are:

The Anti-Marcionite Prologue (c. 160-180).[3]

> . . . Mark declared, who is called "stumped-fingered," because he had rather small fingers in comparison with the stature of the rest of his body. He was the interpreter of Peter. After the death of Peter he wrote down this same gospel in the region of Italy.

Irenaeus (end of second century):

> And after the death of these (Peter and Paul), Mark, the disciple and interpreter of Peter, also transmitted to us in writing the things preached by Peter.

Origen (+ 254)

> And second, that according to Mark, who did as Peter instructed him, whom also he acknowledged as a son in the Catholic Epistle in these words: "She that is in Babylon, who is likewise chosen, sends you greetings, as does Mark my son." (I Pet. 5, 13).

The verdict of modern scholarship on the traditional evidence may be summed up in the words of an eminent non-Catholic scholar: "There can be no doubt that the author of the Gospel was Mark, the attendant of Peter. This is the unbroken testimony of the earliest Christian opinion from Papias onwards. In an age when the tendency of Christian tradition was to assign the authorship of the Gospels to Apostles, Mark is not likely to have been named as the author unless there was very good reason to make that claim." [4]

2. New Testament Witness to St. Mark

Tradition names St. Mark, the interpreter and disciple of Peter, as the author of the second gospel. This is the same Mark who is frequently mentioned in the New Testament. [5]

(i) *Acts* speaks six times of a person variously called "John surnamed Mark" (12, 12.25; 15, 37) or "John" (13, 5.13) or "Mark" (15, 39). It is the same person in each case. The companion "John surnamed Mark" whom Barnabas and Paul took with them from Jerusalem to Antioch (12, 25) is no other than the helper called "John" who later accompanied them on the first missionary journey (13, 5) and who left them shortly afterwards (13, 13). On the other hand the "John surnamed Mark" who was the occasion of the separation of Barnabas and Paul (15, 37) is evidently the "Mark" with whom Barnabas returned to Cyprus (15, 39).

(ii) In the *Epistles* of St. Paul the name is mentioned three times, always in the form "Mark": Col. 4, 10 (where he is described as the cousin of Barnabas); Philemon 24; II Tim. 4, 11. When these texts are compared it is certain that the same person is meant in each case.

(iii) *I Pet. 5, 13*. Peter sends his readers the greeting of "Mark my son." In *Acts* 12, 12-17, Peter, delivered from prison, went straight to the house of Mary the mother of "John surnamed Mark." It is natural to suppose that Peter had baptized the family and that Mark was thus his spiritual son.

From this New Testament evidence the following picture emerges: The Mark whom Peter calls his "son" (I Pet. 5,

13), and who was with him in Rome when the epistle was written, is the same whose family the Apostle knew quite well (Acts 12, 12). It is the same Mark who accompanied Paul and Barnabas on their first missionary journey (Acts 12, 25; 13, 5.13) and who was later the occasion of a quarrel between them (Acts 15, 37.39). But we find him again with Paul during the latter's first captivity (Philemon 24; Col. 4, 10), and the Apostle sent for him during his second captivity (II Tim. 4, 11). His Jewish name was John, and the form John Mark is explained by the assumption of a Greek surname—a frequent practice of Jews throughout the Roman Empire.

The fact that Mark, who had been the cause of a misunderstanding between Paul and Barnabas, should later be the trusted companion of Paul, raises no difficulty. It is readily understandable too that Mark, who was first in contact with Peter, should be the disciple of Paul in the years 44-46 and later in 60-63, to be again the disciple of Peter about 63-64. The New Testament texts which refer to St. Mark are all the more striking since there is no suggestion of harmonization. It follows that the evangelist was in the very best position to know the catechesis of Peter, both in Jerusalem and in Rome, and he was also aware of the preaching of Paul.[6]

3. Destination and Date

The gospel of St. Mark was written for non-Jewish Christians. This is evident from the explanation of Aramaic expressions (e.g., "Boanerges, that is, sons of thunder" 3, 17; " 'Talitha cum,' which means, 'Little girl, I say to you, arise' " 5, 41. Cf. 7, 11.34; 14, 36; 15, 22.34), as well as of Jewish customs (7, 3 f; 14, 12; 15, 42).

According to early tradition the gospel was written in Rome. The many Latinisms in Mark may, in the main, be written off as current military and technical terms, but there are two striking occasions when a Greek expression is explained by its Latin equivalent: "two lepta (Greek coins), that is, a quadrans (Roman coin)" 12, 42; the "interior of the palace, that is, the praetorium" 15, 16. These would suggest that the gospel was written in Rome.

St. John Chrysostom says that Mark was written in
Egypt, but this claim cannot be reconciled with the words
of Clement of Alexandria and of Origen, and is probably
due to the misunderstanding of an ambiguous statement
of the Church historian Eusebius. Antioch is also mentioned.
But the weight of evidence, supported by internal criticism,
that is to say, the study of the gospel itself, is over-
whelmingly in favor of the Roman origin of Mark.

It is almost unanimously agreed that the gospel was
written before the year 70 (the date of the destruction of
Jerusalem by the Romans). We have the testimony of
Irenaeus and the Anti-Marcionite Prologue to the effect that
St. Mark wrote after the death of Peter (c. 64); we cannot
be far wrong if we date the gospel 64-65.

VIII

Literary Construction of the Second Gospel

1. Plan of the Gospel

Part I.
I.   Introduction 1, 1-13.

II. The Galilean Ministry 1, 14-3, 6.
   1. Opening Summary Statement 1, 14 f.
   2. Call of the First Disciples 1, 16-20.
   3. *The Ministry at Capharnaum* 1, 21-39.
   4. The Cure of a Leper 1, 40-45.
   5. *Conflicts with the Scribes* 2, 1-3, 6.

III. The Height of the Galilean Ministry 3, 7-6, 13.
   1. Summary Statement: Crowds by the Lake 3, 7-12.
   2. Appointment of the Twelve 3, 13-19a.
   3. *Charges brought against Christ* 3, 19b-35.
   4. *Parabolic Teaching* 4, 1-34.
   5. *A Group of Miracle-stories* 4, 35-5, 43.
   6. Rejection at Nazareth 6, 1-6a.

IV. The Close of the Galilean Ministry 6, 6b-7, 23.
   1. The Mission Charge to the Twelve 6, 6b-13.

In this plan the longer sections of continuous narrative (1, 21-39; 4, 35-5, 43; 6, 30-56; 7, 24-37; 8, 27-9, 29) stand out—it seems that here special information was available to the evangelist. At the same time it would also appear that the passages 2, 1-3, 6; 3, 19b-35; 4, 1-34; 7, 1-23; 11, 27-12, 44 are units which St. Mark found already formed and which he preserved intact, for it is apparent that these interrupt or halt the course of events. So, for example, 3, 19b-35 (though this does not, of course, affect its intrinsic worth) comes as an anti-climax after 2, 1-3, 6 and the latter section, in turn, (cf 3, 6) occurs too early in the gospel.

However, these stylistic shortcomings really add to the historical value of Mark. A more gifted writer would have arranged things differently and the gospel would have been improved from the literary point of view. But in the process it would have lost something of inestimable value, its close link with the earlier tradition. As it stands, its arrangement can best be understood if it is seen that St. Mark has preserved, more or less intact, traditional groupings that were already familiar to his first readers.

Though, on the whole, the plan of Mark is not very systematic, it does follow the main lines of the primitive catechesis.[2] The prelude (1, 1-13) deals with the preaching of John the Baptist, the Baptism of our Lord and the Temptations. Then follows a period of ministry in Galilee (1, 14-7, 23), and after that come journeys to Tyre and Sidon and to Decapolis, with a return to Galilee. The confession of Peter at Caesarea Philippi is a cardinal point— even in the sense that here the gospel swings apart and is divided in two. Hitherto Jesus had appeared as the Messiah, but now the Passion is in view; henceforth he is a suffering Messiah who goes to his death. Though there is a return to Galilee (9, 30-50), in reality the final journey to Jerusalem begins after the descent from the mount of Transfiguration (9, 2-8), the journey that ends in the Passion and Resurrection.

Corresponding to the division of the gospel there is a development in the self-manifestation of Jesus. At first— during the Galilean ministry—he taught the people. He spoke openly, in a manner that was congenial to his hearers, by means of parables. Yet this teaching gave only an outline of his message and he took care to explain it more fully to those whose task it would be to preach to all men after his Resurrection.[3] There is also the fact of the reaction of his hearers to be considered. At first he was favorably received by the crowds, but his humble and spiritual Messianism disappointed their hopes and enthusiasm waned, and so, in the second period, he turned to his disciples and devoted himself almost exclusively to their formation. We can say, then, that despite a few inconsistencies—due to the fact that the evangelist was using pre-existing material—the plan of Mark does correspond, very closely, to the historical course of events.

2. Sources of the Gospel

We have already indicated that Mark is based on literary sources, yet the gospel, as we know it, is clearly the work of a single author, for the method of construction and the style are consistent throughout. The Greek is quite unpretentious, even poor; the gospel is full of Aramaisms and there are not a few Latinisms to be found in it. A striking feature is the curious blend of dry stereotyped phrases and vivid details. St. Mark was in no sense an imaginative writer, and he was far from being a skilful writer, yet his work has an undeniable individuality. For all that, perhaps because of it, the problem of the sources of Mark is not an easy one.

One of the best treatments of the question is that by L. Vaganay.[4] In his view Mark is dependent on two main sources:

(i) A Greek translation of Aramaic Matthew. This is a schematized condensation of the apostolic preaching or, in other words, it is, essentially, the Palestinian catechesis of Peter.

(ii) The Roman catechesis of Peter. This is basically the same as the other, but it includes the vivid touches, found throughout Mark, that can only be due to an eyewitness.

The reasonableness of this view becomes apparent when we examine the Markan passages that find parallels in Matthew and Luke. Three different types of these may be distinguished:

(i) Passages which contain picturesque touches not found, or rarely found, in Matthew and Luke. These give a special coloring to the Markan narrative. E.g., 2, 1-12; 4, 35-41.

(ii) Passages which differ very little from those of Matthew and Luke—here there is rarely any personal note in Mark. This type is most frequent in the discourses. E.g., 4, 1-34.

(iii) Markan passages which are manifestly abbreviations, by comparison with Matthew and Luke. E.g., 1, 4-13,

The problem that is raised is how to explain the blend of such sections which have clearly differing characteristics.

Now that difficulty can be solved by taking into account the influence of the two main sources: the Roman and Palestinian catecheses of Peter. The stylized passages, very like those of Matthew in parallel passages, come from a Greek translation of Aramaic Matthew—which is, in fact, a condensed form of the apostolic preaching in Jerusalem. In the passages with more vivid touches the influence is that of the Roman catechesis of Peter. In this the schematic framework is still that of the original Aramaic gospel, but it is understandable that Peter would not have been satisfied with the bare bones of the simplified gospel, and would have added his own reminiscences. And, in fact, the lifelike touches that abound in the gospel can only be due to St. Mark's familiarity with the living preaching of Peter. As for the abbreviated passages, some of them may have had that form in the Aramaic gospel, while others were undoubtedly condensed by St. Mark himself. Thus the problem of the sources of Mark can be satisfactorily solved by recourse to the traditional data: the existence of an original Aramaic gospel, and the fact that St. Mark was a disciple of Peter.

It will be helpful to consider more closely the influence of St. Peter, and a study of the gospel does show that this influence—that of an eyewitness—is very marked.[5] When he preached the gospel Peter heard again the familiar voice of Jesus, and saw him move again before his eyes—all this comes through in Mark. Peter saw not only Jesus but also those who were associated with Him, and that is why, in this gospel particularly, not only the Lord, but the other personages too, are people of flesh and blood, and always it is very simple touches, details of everyday occurrence, that bring them vividly to life.

At the call of Jesus the sons of Zebedee rose up and followed him, and their father was left in the boat "with the hired servants" (1, 20). On the evening of the first sabbath spent at Capharnaum "the whole village was gathered about the door of the house" (1, 33) where Jesus was staying. At other times there was such a concourse of people that he and his disciples had no time to eat (6, 31). The sick man who was brought on his bed to Jesus was "carried by four men" (2, 3). The accounts of the cure of the deaf-mute and of the blind man at Bethsaida abound in details that were seen and remembered: Jesus putting his fingers in the ears of the deaf man and touching his tongue with spittle and exclaiming: "Ephphatha" (7, 33-34) and the spontaneous remark of the blind man when he began to regain his sight: "I see men, but they look like trees, walking" (8, 24). On the way to Jerusalem for the Passion, Christ walked in front of his disciples (10, 32). When he sent two of his disciples to procure a donkey they found the colt tied at a door out in the open street (11, 4). There is, too, the unforgettable picture of Jesus, during the storm on the lake, lying asleep on a cushion at the stern of the boat. (4, 38).—These are only a few of the details that make the Markan narratives so delightful. In every case we can, behind the prose of Mark, discern the accents of the Prince of the Apostles.

3. Pre-existing Literary Units

Scholars are agreed that much of St. Mark's material was found already grouped in units, and the evangelist merely reproduced many of these complexes. This view is in full accord with the picture that emerged from our consideration of the formation of the gospels.[6] In the second stage of the formation the first written accounts appeared, that is to say, certain groupings of sayings and narratives were set down in writing. We find proof of these literary units in Mark; but the evangelist, in his turn, found them already grouped, in his principal source—the apostolic catechesis. It will be helpful to look more closely at some of these.

In Mark 2, 1-36 we have a series of five conflicts of Christ with the Pharisees, in Galilee: on forgiveness of sins (2, 1-12); on eating with publicans and sinners (2, 13-17); on fasting (2, 18-22; concerning the plucking of ears on the sabbath (2, 23-28); concerning healing on the sabbath (3, 1-6). These are arranged in progressive order. At the cure of the paralytic the opposition is latent, the scribes "questioned in their hearts" (2, 6-7). During the meal in the house of Levi they addressed the disciples, though they were really attacking the Master (2, 16). With regard to fasting they questioned Jesus about an omission of his disciples (2, 18), but in the case of the ears on the sabbath the charge is a direct violation of the law (2, 24). In the last episode the adversaries spy on Christ (3, 2) and then meet in council to plot his destruction (3, 6). This last point makes it clear that we are dealing with a pre-existing arrangement, one which emphasized the growing opposition to Christ, for such official action against him did not take place so early in the ministry, and the plot is not mentioned again until much later (11, 18; 12, 12). It is obvious that St. Mark has reproduced the unit just as he found it, and decided to insert it at this point in his gospel.

Further on we come across another series of five conflicts which seems to correspond to the other. These centre around: the mission of Jesus and the Baptism of John (11, 27-33)—the parable of the Wicked Husbandmen (12, 1-12) has been inserted at this point—the tribute to Caesar (12, 13-17); the resurrection (12, 18-27); the greatest commandment (12, 28-34); the origin of the Messiah (12, 35-37). Again it is a question of narratives already grouped before they took their place in the gospel. It is noteworthy that the "Herodians" are mentioned by the evangelist twice only, and then in the context of these conflicts: 3, 6 and 12, 13.[7]

Having thus illustrated what we mean by pre-existing units we can set about classifying them.[8] The importance of this step is that the recognition of different kinds of traditional material, and the evangelist's use of it, will enable us to explain a certain lack of logical order in Mark, and, what is more important, it will take us back beyond the gospel to an earlier stage of the tradition. The following classification has the advantage of being rather general, because, in these matters, we cannot be too precise.

(i) Groups of narratives based on personal testimony, most probably that of Peter:

1, 21-39; 4, 35-5, 43; 6, 30-56; 7, 24-37; 8, 27-9, 29.

These are groups of vivid narratives that are linked together by statements which fix them at a given time or place. St. Mark fitted them into his general plan as simply as he could.

(ii) Groups containing sayings and pronouncement-stories.[9] 2, 1-3, 6; 3, 20-35; 4, 1-34; 7, 1-23; 11, 27-12, 37; 13, 1-37.

In all these the center of interest is a saying of Jesus, and the groups were compiled in order to make his mind known on matters of vital importance to the Christian community.

(iii) Less well-defined groups.

1, 1-13; 3, 13-19; 6, 6-13; 9, 30-11, 25.

These also seem to indicate previous groupings of material in the oral period or, perhaps, more accurately, in the period of the first written accounts.

(iv) Summary statements.

The gospel contains a number of summaries which describe the activity of our Lord over a period, and which sketch the course of events. The two most striking of these are 1, 14-15 which indicates the opening of the public ministry and gives the theme of the preaching of Jesus, and 3, 7-12 which describes the external features of the ministry Cf. also 1, 21f.39; 2, 13; 6, 7.12f.30, etc.

In this context we may consider a notable tendency in Mark, that of schematization, or the casting of narratives, miracle-stories especially, in the one mold. For example, here are two distinct and quite different miracles described according to the same pattern and in almost identical terms.[10]

THE TEMPEST STILLED (4, 39-41)	AN EXORCISM (1, 25-27)
And he awoke and *rebuked* the wind	*And* Jesus *rebuked* him
and *said to the sea*	*saying*
"*Be silent,* be still"	"*Be silent,* and go out of him"
(Effect of the command:	(Effect of the command:

the sea stilled)	cure of the possessed person)
And they were filled with awe	And they were all amazed, so that
and *said* to one another	they questioned one another, *saying*
Who then is this?	*What* is this?

In this same way we can compare the cure of the blind man at Bethsaida (8, 22-26) and that of the deaf-mute (7, 32-36); the preaching of Jesus in his own country (6, 1-2) and in Capharnaum (1, 26-27); the preparation of the Supper (14, 13-16) and the entry into Jerusalem (11, 1-6).

It is clear that frequently the same, or a similar framework, has been used for different narratives. This stereotyped construction may possibly be the work of the evangelist, but it can be most reasonably explained by seeking its origin in the oral teaching. Admittedly, the preaching of Christ was very personal, and the teaching of the Apostles must have been modeled on that of the Master. But, as time passed, it was necessary to make a résumé of the words and works of Jesus for the use of missionaries; it was then that the schematized narratives appeared.[11]

From all this we get some idea of how St. Mark worked. He was content to take the pre-existing material and fit it in, as best he could, into his own plan. This plan itself was essentially that of the apostolic catechesis, and went back, like the Aramaic gospel which was his main written source, through the intermediary stages, to the oral tradition. In Mark we see most clearly the true role of an evangelist. The gospel is not a private undertaking and the evangelist is only the last link in a chain. Behind him stand the preachers and the Apostles, the whole teaching activity of a living Church. The gospel, founded on the words and works of Christ, was lived in the Church, and the evangelist, though himself directly inspired by God, is also the spokesman of a Church guided by the Spirit of God.

4. Language and Style of Mark

Mark is written in a relatively simple and popular form

of Greek that has striking affinities with the spoken language of everyday life, as it is otherwise known to us. The evangelist is by no means a skilful writer. He uses only the simplest constructions; a glance at the gospel will show that sentences are most often strung together by the simple conjunction "and." Aramaisms[12] abound in his pages, to such an extent indeed that some few have suggested that his gospel was originally written in Aramaic. The great majority of scholars reject this view; one of them has put the position rather neatly: "The strong Semitic coloring of the gospel indicates, not that it is the translation of an Aramaic original, but that its author is Palestinian born and that his mother-tongue is Aramaic." [13]

There are many Latin terms in Mark, mostly of a technical nature, e.g., denarius, legion, centurion. The fact that these occur more frequently than in the other gospels, and that on two occasions a Greek expression is explained by its Latin equivalent (12, 42; 15, 16) would suggest that the evangelist wrote in a Roman environment. So, in fact, considerations of language and style support the traditional view of the origin of Mark. The remark of V. Taylor is apposite: "The sympathies of Mark are Gentile in their range, but his tradition is Jewish Christian to the core."

A point to be borne in mind when examining the style of Mark is the limitation imposed on the evangelist by the earlier groupings of gospel material. He wished to retain many of these unbroken and thereby was not in a position to write freely. He had to fit them into his general plan as best he could and very often the artificiality of the result is manifest. "The apparently poor literary style of St. Mark is often only a manifestation of his fidelity to his sources. This must certainly be taken into account when judging the merits of his work." [14]

St. Mark's gospel was long regarded as no more than an abridged version of Matthew, and for that reason it was rather neglected, and has not come into its own until recent times. Today it is clearly recognized that it is in no way an abridgement of Matthew; if anything the opposite may be true in some few cases: Mark stands on its own merits.

Still, Mark is quite obviously much shorter than the other Synoptics. We note at once just how few of the sayings of our Lord are found in it. There are three discourses only, and all of them are very brief: the discourse in parables (4, 1-34), the ecclesiastical discourse (9, 33-50) and the eschatological discourse (13, 1-37). It seems that St. Mark has consciously omitted the Sermon on the Mount.[15] On the other hand, in narratives common to the three Synoptics, Mark is usually richer in detail and more picturesque. We have a striking example of this in the account of the raising of the daughter of Jairus; it is certainly quite plain that St. Mark is not abbreviating in this case.[16] We may illustrate the point by giving the texts of the three Synoptics.

> While he was speaking to them, behold a ruler came and knelt before him saying: "My daughter has just died; but come and lay your hand on her and she will live." Jesus rose and followed him, with his disciples. And behold, a woman who had suffered from hemorrhages for twelve years, came up behind him and touched the fringe of his cloak. For she said to herself: "If I only touch his cloak, I shall be cured." Jesus, turning, saw her and said: "Have confidence, my daughter, your faith has saved you." And from that moment the woman was cured. And when Jesus had come to the ruler's house and saw the flute players, and the crowd making a tumult, he said: "Go away; the little girl is not dead: she is asleep." And they laughed at him. But when the crowd had been put outside, he went in and took her by the hand, and the little girl arose. And word of it spread throughout all that country (Matt. 9, 18-26).

> On his return Jesus was welcomed by the crowd, for they were all expecting him. And behold, there came a man named Jairus, who was a ruler of the

synagogue, and throwing himself at the feet of Jesus
he besought him to come to his house, for he had
an only daughter, about twelve years old, and she
was dying. While he was on his way there the people
thronged around him. And a woman who had had a
flow of blood for twelve years, and whom no one
had been able to cure, came up behind him and
touched the fringe of his cloak, and instantly her
flow of blood ceased. And Jesus asked: "Who has
touched me?" As all denied it, Peter said: "Master,
there are crowds thronging about you!" But Jesus replied: "Somebody touched me, for I have felt that
power has gone forth from me." And when the
woman saw that she was detected she came trembling,
and falling down before him, declared before all
the people for what reason she had touched him, and
how she had been instantly cured. And he said to her:
"My daughter, your faith has saved you; go in peace."

While he was still speaking, someone came from the
house of the ruler of the synagogue to tell him: "Your
daughter has died; do not trouble the Master further." Jesus, on hearing this, said to him: "Do not
fear, only have faith and she will be saved." When he
arrived at the house he allowed nobody to go in with
him except Peter and James and John and the
father and mother of the child. All were weeping
and lamenting for her. He said: "Do not weep, she
is not dead, she sleeps." But they laughed at him,
knowing well that she was dead. But he, taking her
hand, called her, saying: "Child, arise." Her spirit
returned and she rose up at once; and he directed that
she should be given something to eat. Her parents
were amazed, but he forbade them to tell anyone
what had happened (Luke 8, 40-56).

And when Jesus had crossed again in the boat
to the other shore, a great crowd gathered round him,
and he was beside the sea. And one of the rulers
of the synagogue, named Jairus, came, and when he
saw him, fell at his feet and pleaded with him ear-

nestly: "My little daughter is at the point of death; come and lay your hands on her that she may be cured and live." And he went with him, and a large crowd followed him and thronged about him.

And a woman who had had a flow of blood for twelve years, and who had suffered much at the hands of many doctors, and had spent all that she had without getting any better, but rather had grown worse, having heard what was said about Jesus, coming up behind him in the crowd, touched his cloak. For she said to herself: "If I touch even his clothes, I shall be cured." And instantly the source of the flow was dried up, and she felt in her body that she was cured of her trouble. And immediately Jesus was aware that power had gone out from him, and turning round in the crowd, he asked: "Who touched my clothes?" And his disciples said to him: "You see the crowd pressing upon you on all sides and you ask: 'Who touched me'!" And he looked around to see who had done it. Then the woman, in fear and trembling, knowing well what had happened to her, came and fell at his feet and told him the whole truth. He said to her: "My daughter, your faith has made you well; go in peace and be free from this complaint of yours."

While he was still speaking messengers came from the house of the ruler of the synagogue to tell him: "Your daughter is dead; why trouble the Master any further?" But Jesus, having overheard the message that was delivered, said to the ruler of the synagogue: "Do not fear, only believe." And he would allow nobody to accompany him except Peter and James, and John the brother of James. And they arrived at the house of the ruler of the synagogue, and he saw a tumult and people weeping and wailing loudly. And when he entered he said to them: "Why do you make a tumult and weep? The child is not dead but sleeping." And they laughed at him. But when he had sent them all out, he took with him the father and mother of the child and those who were with him, and went in where the child was. And taking the hand of the child he said to her: *"Talitha cum,"* which means, "Little girl, I say to you, arise." Immediately the little girl got up and walked about, for she was twelve years old. And they were immediately overcome with amazement. And he strictly charged them that no one should know this, and told them to give her something to eat. (Mark 5, 21-43).[17]

This passage is no isolated case, for there are many other examples, especially in the first part of the gospel. So, for instance, the cure of the paralytic (Mark 2, 1-12; Matt. 9, 1-8; Luke 5, 17-26); the stilling of the tempest (Mark 4, 35-41; Matt. 8, 23-27; Luke 8,22-25); the first multiplication of loaves (Mark 6, 30-44; Matt. 14, 13-21; Luke 9, 10-17). Mark is no abridgement; though it is shorter than Matthew and Luke, that is due to the evangelist's own choice and method, just as it was his choice to record the vivid details he had learned from Peter.

We must not be deceived by the brevity or the simple style of this gospel. Those, even those saints, who neglected Mark because they believed that all of it was to be found in Matthew, were the poorer for their neglect. And we can suitably conclude this section of our study by citing a noble tribute to the evangelist and his gospel.[18]

"In Mark we have an authority of first rank for our knowledge of the Story of Jesus. Separated at the time of writing by little more than a generation from the death of Jesus, its contents carry us back farther into the oral period before Mark wrote to the tradition first of the Palestinian community and subsequently that of the Gentile Church at Rome. The historical value of Mark depends on the Evangelist's fidelity to that tradition, including his special advantage as a hearer of Peter's preaching . . . We may say of the Gospel what St. Paul says of the first missionaries; we have this treasure in earthen vessels, that the exceeding greatness of the power may be of God (II Cor. 4, 7). Without this Gospel, which is not only invaluable in itself, but is also one of the most important sources upon which all the Gospels depend, it is impossible to account for the history of primitive Christianity, or to imagine the perils from which it was preserved; for it sets at the center the personality of Jesus Himself and His redemptive work for men."

Note: The Markan Ending, Mark 16, 9-20

In some of our Mss. of the gospel, the passage 16, 9-20 is omitted. Eusebius and St. Jerome attest that it was wanting in almost all Greek Mss. known to them. Some Mss. have another ending, known as the "Shorter Ending," which is inserted after 16, 8 instead of (or sometimes combined with), 16, 9-20. The Shorter Ending runs:

> And all that has been commanded them they made known briefly to those about Peter. And afterwards Jesus himself appeared to them, and from the East as far as the West sent forth through them the sacred and incorruptible proclamation of eternal salvation.

The vocabulary and style of 16, 9-20 indicate that the passage was not written by St. Mark; it is based on a knowledge of the traditions found in the other gospels, especially in Luke. E.g., in v. 9, Mary Magdalen "from whom he had cast out seven devils" = Luke 8, 2. v. 12, the apparition to two disciples = Luke 24, 13-35. The title "the Lord Jesus" (v. 19) is frequent in *Acts* but is found nowhere else in the gospels.

Possibly St. Mark did not end his work at 16, 8; in that case his closing verses have been lost. It is also suggested that St. Mark may have died before he was able to complete the gospel. At any rate, 16, 9-20 was added at a very early date. Catholics can have no doubt regarding the inspiration of this passage, for it has been accepted by the Church as forming an integral part of Sacred Scripture.

IX
Some Theological Ideas of the Second Gospel

1. The Suffering Messiah

The central theme of St. Mark's gospel is the manifestation of the Suffering Son of God. Like St. Matthew, he sees that Jesus is the Messiah, but he insists more than Matthew on the sufferings of the Messiah. And for him, too, the Messiah is more clearly the Son of God.[1]

In the very first line of his gospel, indeed, St. Mark affirms that Jesus is the Son of God: "The beginning of the gospel of Jesus Christ, the Son of God." (1, 1). At the Baptism, and again at the Transfiguration, the Father acknowledges his Son: "This is my beloved Son." At his trial Christ admits that he is the "Son of the Blessed" (14, 61). He claims the power of forgiving sins (2, 5-11), and when the Pharisees reprove the disciples for plucking ears of corn on the sabbath he tells them that the Son of Man is "lord even of the sabbath" (2, 27-28).

But this Son of God is a Suffering Messiah—that is made clear in the second part of the gospel. The ministry of our Lord in Galilee leads eventually to Caesarea Philippi and to Peter's recognition and acknowledgement of the Messiahship of Jesus. This is a cardinal point. Immediately now the Passion is in view (8, 31) and henceforth it is the Passion that dominates the gospel. Christ sets out on the journey, on the last journey, to Jerusalem. Twice he repeats the prediction of his sufferings, always in more explicit terms—though the evangelist has to add, sadly, that the disciples did not understand (9, 32).

> Behold, we are going up to Jerusalem and the Son of man will be handed over to the high priests and the scribes; and they will condemn him to death and will hand him over to the pagans who will mock him and spit at him and flog him and put him to death. 10, 33-34 (Cf. 9, 30-32).

He and his disciples were on the road traveling up to Jerusalem "and Jesus was walking ahead of them" (10, 32); he was in a hurry to face his Passion and meet his death! For his way led inevitably to the Cross, and the Scriptures had foretold it (9, 12). He *had* to suffer to ransom men:

> For the Son of man did not come to be served, but to serve, and to give his life as a ransom for many (10, 45).

The Christ of St. Mark is Son of God, yet his humanity is evident and he has very human sentiments and emotions. Thus he is moved in the presence of human suffering. When a leper came to him, asking to be healed, "moved with pity," he stretched out his hand and touched him (1, 40-41). He was stirred more deeply by the spiritual ills of men. To the Pharisees, who accused him of contravening their strict laws of ritual purity by dining with publicans and sinners, he said: "It is not the healthy who need a doctor, but the sick; I came not to call the just but sinners" (2, 17). It is the parable of the Lost Sheep all over again.

Once during his Galilean ministry he came to Nazareth and found that a prophet has no honor in his own country, "and he was astounded at their lack of faith" (6, 6). He can be indignant. Children were brought to him that he might touch them, but the disciples turned them away—Jesus saw it, and he was indignant (10, 14). He could be angry too. The Pharisees were watching him to see whether he would heal on the sabbath and he asked them whether it were lawful to do good on the sabbath rather than evil. The answer was obvious, but they refused to be drawn; in bad faith they took refuge in silence. "Then he

looked around at them in anger, grieved at their hardness
of heart" (3, 5). And at Gethsemani he was filled with
shuddering awe at the approach of death. Hitherto he had
gone resolutely to face his Passion, but now, when it was
just at hand, his human nature shrank from suffering and
death.

> He took with him Peter and James and John and
> he began to feel dismayed and desolate. And he said
> to them: "My soul is in anguish to the point of
> death; wait here and keep awake." And going a little
> farther, he threw himself on the ground and prayed
> that if possible the hour might pass from him (14,
> 33-35).

In all these cases, in Gethsemani above all, St. Mark
reminds us that Christ is Man. We see him as he appeared
to the eyes of his disciples, we see him in the reality of
his Incarnation, we see him in our flesh. But we perceive too that the Man of Sorrows is also a Being of
supernatural origin and dignity since he is Son of God.
And Christ is still the Son of God even when he is most
human, even in death. So it is that St. Mark can take the
cry of the awed centurion, and set it down, transformed
now by the certainty of his own faith:

> Truly, this man was Son of God (15, 39).

2. Son of Man

The title "Son of Man" is—because of its use in the
gospels—such a familiar one that we do not advert to
it or to its meaning. And what *does* it mean—Son of
Man? It is, in fact, a literal translation of the Aramaic expression *bar nasha,* which means simply "man." But it is
also capable of conveying the notion "the man," and so
of being used in a special, Messianic sense. As found in
the gospels, the origin of the title goes back to the *Book
of Daniel*. In Dan. 7, 13 the prophet sees in vision:

> Behold, with the clouds of heaven
> there came one like a Son of man;
> he came to the Ancient of Days and was led into his
> presence.
> And he was given dominion and glory and kingdom,

and all peoples, nations and languages shall serve him.
His dominion is an everlasting dominion which shall
    not pass away,
  and his kingdom one that shall not be destroyed.

This mysterious figure is manifestly no ordinary man—
it can only be the Messiah, and indeed, he does appear as
the head of the Messianic people, the Saints of the Most
High (7, 22-27). But, at the same time, this is a conception "which is very different from that of the traditional
Messiah—an earthly king, descended from David, who
conquers his enemies in war. This leader has become a
transcendent personage, of heavenly origin, who receives his
dominion by a sovereign and direct intervention of God." [2]
Even apart from this difference, "Son of Man" was not a
title used by the Jews of the future Messiah[3] as was, for
example, "Son of David." Despite this, or, rather, as we
shall see, precisely because of this, "Son of Man" does
designate the Messiah who had come.

Before turning to the use of "Son of Man" in Mark,
we have to consider another Old Testament concept that is
essentially linked with this title in the gospels. In the
second part of *Isaias*, four poems or canticles may be
regarded as, in some way, distinct from the rest of the
book: 42, 1-7; 49, 1-9; 50, 4-9; 52, 13-53, 12. These have
to do with a mysterious figure called the "Servant of Yahweh." For our purpose the most significant passage is
Isa. 53. This is concerned with the sufferings of the Servant,
and the really noteworthy feature is that the suffering is
vicarious, that is to say, he suffers, and dies, for, and in the
place of, others.

He was despised and aloof from men,
  A man of pains and familiar with suffering . . .
But it was our sufferings that he bore,
  Our pains that he endured . . .
He was wounded for our rebellions,
  He was bruised for our sins;
Upon him was the chastisement which made us whole,
  And by his stripes we were healed . . .
He was afflicted, but he was resigned,

And he opened not his mouth;
Like a lamb that is led to the slaughter,
   And like a ewe that is dumb before its shearers . . .
For he was cut off from the land of the living,
   With the rebellious who are stricken down;
And his grave was assigned among the wicked,
   And his portion with the doers of evil,
Albeit he had done no violence,
   And there was no deceit in his mouth;
And Yahweh was pleased to crush him with suffering
   (53, 3-10).[4]

The Servant is, obviously, an exceptional personage, and, once again, it can only be the Messiah. But, just as in the case of the Son of Man, we do not find that Isa. 53 was currently interpreted in a Messianic sense. Though in some circles the concept of a suffering Messiah may have arisen, yet official Judaism in New Testament times did not regard the Servant of Yahweh in a Messianic light. This is, perhaps, understandable if we realize that for the Jews in general the idea of a Messiah who had to suffer was unthinkable. The gospels, on the other hand, make it clear that Jesus (though he did not designate himself by the title "Servant of Yahweh"), applied to himself the idea of vicarious suffering and death. The Suffering Servant, no less than the heavenly figure of *Daniel*, stands behind the title "Son of Man."

This title, found exclusively in the gospels (with the exception of Acts 7, 56—which refers to the reply of Jesus before the Sanhedrin, Matt. 26, 64—and Apoc. 1, 13; 14, 14—which are explicit references to Dan. 7, 13—), is always a self-designation of Christ. The title occurs fourteen times in Mark and, apart from 2, 10.28, it is found only in the second part of the gospel, subsequently to the confession of Peter at Caesarea Philippi (8, 29). This list is: 2, 10.28; 8, 31.38; 9, 9.12.31; 10, 33.45; 13, 26; 14, 21 (twice). 41.62. In three cases (8, 38; 13, 26; 14, 62) it is the glory of the Son of Man that is envisaged. For instance, during the trial, when the high priest asked our Lord if he were the Messiah, he replied that he was, and added:

> You will see the Son of man sitting at the right hand of the Power and coming with the clouds of heaven. 14, 62.

—this is almost a citation of Dan. 7, 13. Elsewhere (always excepting 2, 10.28) the sufferings of the Son of Man are in question. Thus, after Peter's confession we read:

> And he began to teach them that the Son of man must suffer much, and be rejected by the elders and the high priests and the scribes, and be put to death, and after three days, rise. 8, 31.

This and related texts look to the Suffering Servant of Isa. 53, the Man of Sorrows who bore the iniquity of us all, and who went like a lamb to slaughter.

In short, the title Son of Man occurs in two contexts. It designates: (a) the glorious Christ who will come at the end of the world to judge mankind; (b) Christ, the Suffering Servant, the Man of Sorrows. Jesus, by using this title, linked together the two notions of the great Judge of the world and of the Servant of Yahweh—notions that would seem mutually exclusive—and showed that both were united in his person.

We have yet to consider Mark 2, 10.28. Elsewhere, the title "Son of Man" occurs after the confession of Peter, but 2, 10.28 refer to a time in the beginning of the ministry. On examining these texts we find that in each case a divine prerogative is in question: 2, 10 remission of sins; 2, 28 Lord of the sabbath—and for the Jews these prerogatives were exclusively divine. But Christ laid claim to them, as Son of Man. In these passages Jesus presents himself as a heavenly being; he claims that he has brought down on earth the very source of pardon which hitherto had existed only in heaven: "That you may know that the Son of man has *on earth* the power to forgive sins." He claims the right to dispense the disciples from the divine law of the sabbath observance, and that, in practice, amounts to the declaration that he is introducing a new order in which the sabbath observance will no longer have place.[5] Here no less than elsewhere the title "Son of Man" is most certainly Messianic.

3. The Messianic Secret

Son of Man, then, expresses the complexity and the full-ness of the Messianic idea, but it remains a mysterious title. Why should our Lord have used a mysterious title? In order to answer this question, another feature must be taken into account, one that is found in the other gospels too, but which is most obvious in Mark. [6]

Throughout this gospel our Lord is at pains to hide his Messiahship. The devils know him and cry out: "You are the Son of God"—and he commands them to be silent (1, 25.34; 3, 11 f). Silence is enjoined after notable mira-cles. For instance, after he had raised the daughter of Jairus he turned to those who were present "and he strictly charged them that no one should know this" (5, 43; cf. 1, 44; 7, 36; 8, 26). [7] Again, when at Caesarea Philippi Peter had recognized his Messiahship, and later when he was transfigured before Peter and James and John, he admonished them to tell nobody until he had risen from the dead (8, 30; 9, 9). From time to time he withdrew from the crowd on secret journeys (7, 27; 9, 30). He gave his disciples private instructions (e.g., 4, 10-11, 33-34).

It is clear that our Lord wished to remain in the back-ground, but this attitude is puzzling when one recalls other statements in the gospels. We find that soon after he had begun his ministry, when he had cast out an evil spirit, "immediately his fame spread everywhere, throughout all the countryside of Galilee" (1, 28). At the moment of his arrest he stated quite plainly that he had not hidden himself, but had taught openly in the Temple (14, 48-49).

He taught men and he wanted men to be convinced of the truth of his teaching, and so he worked miracles—and then he forbade them to speak of these miracles! The fact of the matter is that Jesus had to deal with a very real difficulty here. He was indeed the Messiah and he wished to proclaim it, and, on the other hand, the people were eagerly awaiting the coming of the Messiah, but— and this is the whole trouble—they had their own notion of the kind of Messiah they wanted.

The prophets had foretold that he would be a son of David and that his kingdom would last forever. He would

come like a king, then, gloriously, and he would lead the
Jews to victory over their enemies, over the hated Romans
in the first place. He would set up his throne in Jerusalem.
Palestine would be his kingdom, but as the center of a
world empire, and all nations would serve the chosen
people. Such were their grandiose expectations, based on
a too literal interpretation of the figurative language of
the prophets, and fomented by the frustration of the long
years of subjection.

Even the disciples shared these views. (Mark 10, 35-45;
Luke 24, 21). And, on the other hand, the conception of
a Messiah who would suffer and die for the sins of his
people was quite foreign to current Messianic ideas. It is
significant that even when Isa. 53 was interpreted as referring to the Messiah the notion of suffering was explained
away—a feat which called for no little ingenuity! Our Lord
well knew that if he openly claimed to be the Messiah, the
people would look to him to take strong action, or they
would reject him as an imposter. How careful he had to
be is evident from a passage of John. We read that when
he had fed the five thousand the people were greatly
impressed and exclaimed:

> "This is indeed the prophet who is to come into
> the world." And realizing that they were about to
> come and seize him so that they might make him
> king, Jesus fled again to the mountain, all alone (John
> 6, 14-15).

Our Lord was indeed the Messiah, but he could not tell
the people openly because of their false notion of the
Messiah. He was indeed a king, but his kingdom was not
of this world. That is why he imposed silence: Because of
the idea of Messiahship as he conceived it—the spiritual
Messiahship of a suffering Messiah—and because of the
prevalent false notions on the subject. And that is why he
called himself Son of Man. It was not a current Messianic
title but it could, and in fact it did, designate the Messiah.
Under this name he was the King and the great Judge
whom the prophets had foretold, but he was, too, the
Suffering Servant of God. He claimed to be the Messiah

indeed, yet not such a Messiah as the people expected. He was the Messiah that St. Mark presents to us.

Jesus the Messiah is Son of God, Son of Man. Either title enshrouds the mystery of his person, but it was the second that he chose to use, and, in the circumstances, he could not have introduced himself in any clearer terms. While it is probable that in certain circles of Judaism a Messiah was awaited who was "Son of Man," it is certain that this conception of the Messiah was not widespread, and the crowds were manifestly puzzled by the title (Cf. John 12, 34; Mark 8, 27-30). But the Jewish leaders realized that Jesus claimed to be more than the traditional Messiah, and that is the reason why he was accused of blasphemy. "In likening himself to the 'Son of Man' of *Daniel* he gave to the title 'Son of God' itself a meaning that was not metaphorical but proper and transcendent, one that was unacceptable to their strict monotheism. (Cf. Luke 22, 70; John 19, 7; Matt. 27, 40). That is why they decided on his death."[8]

The disciples too must have understood, better than the crowds who listened to him, what "Son of Man" meant. And yet the gospels make it clear that they did not, before his death, really grasp the mystery of his person. "The humanity of Jesus was a veil difficult to pierce. The mystery that surrounded him could not be really lifted while he was still with them as one of themselves. It needed the Passion to make them understand that he was in very truth the suffering Servant who makes atonement for the sins of the world; it needed the Resurrection and the outpouring of the Spirit to convince them that he truly belonged to the divine world."[9]

X
Authorship of
the Third Gospel

1. Testimony of Tradition

The testimony of tradition regarding the authorship of
the third gospel is unhesitating: it is the work of St. Luke.
The chief witnesses are:

Irenaeus (end of second century):
"Luke, the companion of Paul, wrote the latter's gospel
in a book."

Anti-Marcionite Prologue (c. 160-180):
"Luke, a Syrian of Antioch, doctor by profession, was
the disciple of the Apostles. At a later date he was the
disciple of Paul until the death of the latter. After having
served the Lord without fault and never having married,
he died, full of the Holy Spirit, at Boeotia, aged eighty-four.
As gospels had already been written by Matthew in Judea
and by Mark in Italy, Luke, under the impulse of the
Holy Spirit, wrote his gospel in the region of Achaia. In
the prologue he shows that other gospels had been written
before his, but that it was necessary to present to the faithful converted from paganism an exact account of the economy of salvation, lest they should be impeded by Jewish
fables or caused to stray from the truth by the deceits of
heretics."

The Muratorian Canon (end of second century)[1]

Luke, a doctor and companion of Paul, wrote the third gospel. He himself had not seen the Lord.

St. Jerome gives a summary of the traditional data:

"Thirdly, Luke the physician, by nation a Syrian of Antioch, whose praise is in the gospel (cf II Cor 8, 18), and who himself was a disciple of the Apostle Paul, wrote in the region of Achaia and Boeotia, seeking material from the ancients, and, as he admits in his preface, writing rather from hearsay than from eyewitness."

(Present-day scholarship generally is quite satisfied that St. Luke, the disciple and companion of St. Paul, wrote Luke and Acts.)

2. New Testament Witness to St. Luke

Just as in the case of St. Mark, the New Testament also has much to tell us about St. Luke, and, once again, that information is found in the epistles of St. Paul and in the Acts of the Apostles.

(i) The Pauline Epistles

St. Luke is named three times: Col. 4, 14; Philemon 23 f; II Tim. 4, 11.

Col. 4, 14:　　"Greetings to you from Luke, our beloved doctor, and from Demas."

Philemon 23f.:　"Epaphras, my co-prisoner in Christ Jesus, greets you; so do Mark, Aristarchus, Demas and Luke, my fellow-workers."

II Tim. 4, 11.:　"I have no one with me but Luke."

Thus, according to Colossians and Philemon Luke was with Paul in Rome during the latter's first captivity (61-63) and according to II Timothy he was with him during the second Roman captivity (67). In Col. 4, 10-14 the collaborators of Paul are divided into two groups: (a) Aristarchus, Mark and Justus, "the only circumcised," i.e., Jews. (b) Epaphras, Luke and Demas, who, by implication, are of pagan origin.

The designation "beloved doctor" (Col, 4, 14) reveals that Luke belonged to an educated class, and also that his services were appreciated by Paul, especially during the second captivity.

(ii) The Acts of the Apostles

The "we-passages": 16, 10-17; 20, 5-15; 21, 1-18; 27, 1-28, 16. In these sections the author of Acts (who, beyond all reasonable doubt, is St. Luke) writes in the first person—hence the designation *"we*-passages"—obviously as an eyewitness. We gather that Luke met Paul at Troas (on the north-west coast of Asia Minor, not far from ancient Troy) during the latter's second missionary journey (50-52). He went to Macedonia with him, to Philippi, where St. Paul founded a church (16, 10-17). Luke appears to have remained at Philippi because the next "we-passage" occurs in the context of the third missionary journey (53-58). Luke joined Paul at Philippi about 57 (20, 5-15) and went with him to Jerusalem; 21, 1-18 deals with the journey from Miletus to Jerusalem, where they were received by James the leader of the Church there. On this occasion Paul was arrested and spent two years as a prisoner at Caesarea, on the Palestinian coast (58-60). This afforded Luke ample time to search out sources, oral and written, both for his gospel and for Acts. He accompanied Paul on the fateful and memorable journey to Rome 60-61 (27, 1-28, 16). There Luke could have met the people mentioned in Col. 4, 10-14 and Philemon 24—especially Mark. Here again the data of the Pauline epistles and of Acts are in perfect accord, and it is clear how a disciple of Paul came to know the Palestinian catechesis of Peter.

3. Destination and Date

St. Luke dedicated his gospel (and Acts) to a certain Theophilus. The title given to him (*kratiste*—Excellency) indicates a man of high social standing. According to ancient custom the man to whom a book was dedicated was expected to promote its circulation.[3]

St. Luke certainly wrote for Gentile Christians—this is quite evident from a study of his gospel. Thus he consistently avoids many matters which might appear too specifically Jewish. He omits whole passages: the traditions of the ancients (Mark 7, 1-23); the return of Elias (Mark 9, 11-13); the opposition between the Old Law and the New (Matt. 5, 21-22.27f. 33-37). Sometimes, instead of suppressing a passage he rearranges it or omits details. For instance, compare Matt. 5, 38-48 with Luke 6, 27-36; Matt. 7, 24-27 with Luke 6, 47-49. He is also careful to omit or play down anything that might shock his Gentile Christian readers: sayings liable to be misunderstood— "About that day or hour no one knows . . . not even the Son" (Mark 13, 32); and the cry from the Cross; "My God, My God, why hast thou forsaken me?" (Mark 15, 34); sentiments of Christ like anger, indignation, sorrow— Compare: "And he looked around at them with anger, grieved at their hardness of heart" (Mark 3, 5) with "And he looked around on them all" (Luke 6, 10). Cf. Luke 19, 45f and Mark 11, 15-17; Luke 22, 39-46 and Mark 14, 32-42; anything which might cast doubt on the omnipotence of Christ—Compare "And he could do no mighty work there (in his own country) . . . and he marveled at their unbelief" (Mark 6, 5-6) with Luke 4, 25-30. Cf. Luke 4, 40 and Mark 1, 34; Luke 5, 15f and Mark 1, 45.

St. Luke also omits or changes details that do not redound to the credit of the Apostles: he has omitted Mark 4, 13; 8, 22f; 9, 10.28f.33f. Elsewhere has has modified the text of Mark: See Luke 8, 24f and Mark 4, 38.40; Luke 18, 25f and Mark 10, 24-26; Luke 22, 31-34 and Mark 14, 27-31. This conduct of St. Luke is explained by Father Lagrange:[8] "Luke, because he was addressing Gentiles, especially Greeks prone to discussions and criticism, did not wish to raise difficulties for them . . . He felt that the transition from the Semitic to the Greek world of ideas would be rendered easier by saying nothing about matters difficult to understand."

Some scholars date Luke 60-62. One of their arguments is that this date is demanded by the date of Acts. Since in the latter writing (they say), St. Luke gives no indication of the outcome of Paul's appeal to Caesar, it follows that Acts must have been written before 63—the end of

Paul's first captivity. The gospel is certainly earlier, so it must have been written about 60-62.

This argument, however, cannot be taken as proving its point. To do so it would have to show that St. Luke intended to give the result of Paul's appeal to Caesar. In fact, the plan of Acts shows that this lay beyond Luke's purpose, and that the ending of the book is indeed just as it should be. St. Luke indicates the plan of Acts by quoting Christ's own words before his ascension: "You will receive power when the Holy Spirit has come upon you, and you will bear witness to me in Jerusalem and in all Judea and in Samaria and to the ends of the earth." (1, 8). St. Luke followed that plan, and at the close— having traced the expansion of the Church from Jerusalem —he has led the great Apostle of the Gentiles to the capital of the Roman Empire, the center of the world, and there, although technically a prisoner, Paul was "preaching the kingdom of God and teaching about the Lord Jesus Christ quite openly and unhindered" (28, 31). This is a masterly ending to a book that has shown the triumphal advance of Christianity and is one more proof of the literary artistry of St. Luke. That, then, is obviously the ending that Luke intended. To say that Acts does not go on to give the outcome of Paul's appeal to Caesar is therefore not a proof that Acts, and consequently Luke, was written before 63.

Some scholars[4] would put the composition of Luke in the decade 70-80. Their main reason for doing so is based on the detailed form of the prediction of the destruction of Jerusalem (19, 43f; 21, 20.24; 23, 28-30). But again, this cannot be taken as a conclusive argument. What, then, of the date of Luke? We had already seen that the most likely date for Mark is 64-65; Luke has followed Mark and must consequently be later.

In the long run the exact date of Luke, apart from being uncertain, is hardly a vital question. "The matter of date is of little importance because nowadays it is seen that the question has no bearing, direct or even indirect, on matters of faith and morals."[5]

XI
Literary Construction of the Third Gospel

1. Plan of the Gospel

A. From the Temple to the Close of the Galilean Ministry.
Prologue 1, 1-4.

C.   Last Days of the Suffering and Risen
      Christ in Jerusalem.

St. Luke, like St. Matthew and St. Mark, has followed
the original fourfold gospel plan; but he has made two
important changes in this order and so has given to his
gospel quite a different bias. By placing at the beginning
the long Infancy-narrative (1-2)—which balances the
Passion and Resurrection narrative—he has presented the
story of Jesus in perfect equilibrium. By his insertion of
the long section (9, 51-18, 14) he has fitted cleverly into
the gospel narrative a very important collection of episodes
and sayings which are entirely absent from Mark and
only partially represented in Matthew. This Lukan section
is dominated by the perspective of the Passion and the
journey to Jerusalem is seen as a journey to death (Cf. 9,
51; 13, 22; 17, 11.) In Luke the story of Jesus falls into
three parts:

(i) From the Temple to the Close of the Galilean
Ministry 1, 5-9, 50.

(ii) The Journey from Galilee to Jerusalem 9, 51-19, 27.

(iii) The Last Days of the Suffering and Risen Christ
in Jerusalem 19, 28-24, 53.

Thus, despite the general agreement with Matthew and
Mark, the third gospel has a distinctive character. The main
division is very clear but it is not so easy to give satisfactory

arrangement of the details, and that is why the plan given
above is rather complicated. It respects a complexity that
really exists and does not seek to falsify the picture by over-
simplification.

2. The Sources of Luke

It is universally recognized that St. Luke has used Mark
as a source, indeed that Mark is his chief source, and he has
manifestly followed the order of Mark. We may put the
relationship between them in schematic form.[1]

		Luke	*Mark*
Prologue		1-2	—
		⎡ 3, 1-6, 19	——>1, 1-3, 19
		⎢ —	3, 20-35
A. In Galilee	⎧	6, 20-8, 3	—
3, 1-9, 50	⎨	8, 4-9, 50	——>4, 1-6, 44 + 8, 27-9, 40,
		⎣ —	6, 45-8, 26
B. To Jerusalem	⎰	9, 51-18, 14	—
9, 5-19, 27	⎱	18, 15-19, 27	——>10, 13-52
C. In Jerusalem		19, 28-24, 53	——>11, 1-16, 8 (20)

The chief differences that meet the eye are (apart from
the omission of Mark 6, 45-8, 26) the additions made by
St. Luke: 6, 20-8, 3 and especially 9, 51-18, 14. It is instructive to see how this last section has, in fact, been
inserted into the order of Mark. In Luke 9, 18-10, 50 and
Mark 8, 27-9, 40 the sequence of events is: profession of
faith by Peter; first prediction of the Passion; the following
of Jesus; the Transfiguration; the epileptic; the second
prediction of the Passion; who is the greatest?; use of the
name of Jesus. At this point St. Luke makes the long
insertion of almost nine chapters. At the end of it (18, 15)
he takes up the plan of Mark again, almost where he had
left off, so that in Luke 18, 15-43 and Mark 10, 13-52
the sequence is: Jesus and children; the rich young man;
the danger of riches; detachment rewarded; the third
prediction of the Passion; the blind man at Jericho.

While it is undoubtedly, and indeed obviously, true that

Luke follows Mark, there is room for a distinction. For Luke, as we have seen,[2] also uses a Greek translation of the original Aramaic gospel—as does Mark. Hence it may not always be correct to say that where Luke and Mark agree Luke is following Mark, for it may be that both are following a common source. But this is, perhaps a subtlety which need not trouble us unduly here.

Of greater interest, and importance, is another source of Luke. We may turn again to Luke 9, 51-18, 14. In this part of his gospel the author has grouped "under the sign of Jerusalem and the Passion," and in no strict chronological order, a great bulk of material which did not come to him via Mark or the Aramaic gospel, whereas, and this is the really significant point, many of these elements are found in Matthew also. The only reasonable explanation is that, besides Aramaic Matthew, another common source was known to St. Matthew and St. Luke. We have seen[3] that this common source may be described as a supplement to the Aramaic gospel.

When we analyze Luke 9, 51-18, 14 we find that we may distinguish: (a) Elements common to Matthew and Luke and absent from Mark; (b) Elements common to Matthew, Mark and Luke.[4]

With regard to (a). There are thirty-three of these elements, for the most part of only a few verses each, and, in general, they are simply sayings. E.g., Luke 13, 24 = Matt. 7,13f; Luke 14, 16-24 = Matt. 22, 1-10; Luke 10, 13-15 = Matt 11, 21-23. It is noteworthy that the resemblances between Matthew and Luke in these passages are relatively more numerous than in pasages common to all three Synoptics. It is clear that in these cases Matthew and Luke follow a common source.

The material indicated under (b) is of much greater significance, for here we have the question of doublets. By doublets we mean the passages—in most cases they consist of sayings—which are met with more than once in the same gospel but in a different context. Some of these may be due to reptition, but many of them point to the use of different sources. An examination of these doublets leads to the conclusion that, in general, in the case of each doublet, the first form of the text appears in parallel passages of the tradition Matthew-Mark-Luke: while the second form, never occurring in Mark, frequent in Matthew and almost always present in Luke 9, 51-18, 14 is in the context of a tradition common to Matthew and Luke. Some examples will clarify this statement:

Saying: "If any man would come after me, let him deny
        himself and take up his cross and follow me."
Mark 8, 34b; Matt. 16, 24b; Luke 9, 23
                         —after the first pre-
                           diction of the
                           Passion.
Matt. 10, 38; Luke 14, 27   —in another context.

Saying: "Whoever would save his life will lose it."
Mark 8, 35; Matt. 16, 25; Luke 9, 24—after the first pre-
                           diction of the
                           Passion.
Matt. 10, 39; Luke 17, 33   —in another context.

Saying: "To him who has it will be given . . ."
Mark 4, 25; Matt. 13, 12; Luke 8, 18—after the parable of
                           the measure.
Matt. 25. 29; Luke 19, 26   —after the parable of
                           the talents (Matt.)
                           and minas (Luke).

The conclusion would seem to be inevitable: Mark has no doublet because it follows one source only (since the contribution of Peter is fundamentally the same as the Aramaic gospel). The agreement of Matthew and Luke, independently of Mark, postulates another and common source. The passages common to the two evangelists make up a collection of sayings and parables; these Matthew has distributed throughout his gospel; while St. Luke has grouped most of them in the long section under review. The three main sources, then, of Luke are: Mark, a Greek translation of Aramaic Matthew, and the special source common to himself and Matthew.

But St. Luke is not confined to these. We know that he had ample time (the two years 58-60) for doing personal research in Palestine, and not only his own prologue ("having followed all these things accurately for some time past"), but a study of the gospel, give abundant proof that he did not waste his time.

First of all there is the Infancy-narrative (1-2), which is proper to Luke and independent of Matthew's first two chapters. The coloring of Luke 1-2 is highly Semitic; it has been suggested that this section is based on a Greek translation of an Aramaic source, while some contend that these chapters were first written in Hebrew. Perhaps the best explanation is this: St. Luke may have had Aramaic sources, but he has written chapters 1-2 of his gospel in a Greek that is modeled on the style of the familiar Greek translation of the Old Testament.[5] these chapters, as they stand, are the work of St. Luke—but where did he get his information? Twice he remarks: "Mary kept all these things, pondering them in her heart." (2, 19.51). Father Lagrange comments that these are two "reserved, but quite clear allusions which give the reader to understand that the Mother of Jesus herself is the source from which the disciples learnt the most intimate secrets of these humble beginnings." [6]

Not only in the Infancy-narrative but throughout his gospel St. Luke presents to us the fruits of his research. One is quite surprised to discover how very much that we had learned to take for granted we owe to St. Luke alone. For instance, the following lovely parables: The Prodigal Son; The Good Samaritain; The Pharisee and the Publican, and the Rich Man and Lazarus are found only in Luke. In the Passion and Resurrection narrative the third gospel has many additions, and it may be well to consider some of these in order to appreciate the extent of our debt.

In 22, 8 it is specified that "John and Peter" were the disciples sent to prepare for the Last Supper; and 22, 11f. tell us of the desire that our Lord felt to celebrate that last Pasch with his disciples. In 22, 35-38 he tells them of the hour of the decisive combat. It is only St. Luke who informs us of the sweat of blood in Gethsemani (22, 43f) and that Jesus healed the wound inflicted by Peter 22, 51). He alone tells (23, 6-16) that our Lord appeared before

Herod, and of the daughters of Jerusalem who wept over Christ (23, 27-31). He only speaks of the pardon of the "good thief" (23, 40-43). While the cry of dereliction on the Cross is not given in this gospel, we find instead three other sayings of our Lord: 23, 34.43.46. And after the Resurrection, it is in Luke that we read of the delightful episode of the disciples on the way to Emmaus (24, 13-35).

St. Luke is an historian and manifestly writes as one.' The careful wording of his prologue and the dedication of his gospel to the "excellent Theophilus" introduce a work that does not purport merely to tell us about the Good News; his object is to establish the soundness of the catechetical teaching and, for that reason, his express intention is to weigh his sources. The prologue shows clearly that St. Luke was conscious of his obligations as an historian.

In view of this he shows great care and accuracy in presenting historical data. Thus, while in Mark we are told that the Transfiguration took place six days after the confession of Peter at Caesarea Philippi (Mark 9, 2). St. Luke quietly modifies that statement and says: "about eight days after" (9, 28); and he regularly qualifies round numbers by adding "about" (1, 56; 3 23 etc). He speaks of Herod as "tetrarch"—his correct title—(9, 7) and not, as he was popularly described, as "king" (Mark 6, 14). Similarly, he speaks of the "lake of Gennesareth" (5, 1) rather than of the "sea of Galilee" (Mark 1, 16). He mentions contemporary facts: the massacre of Galileans by Pilate (13, 1-3) and the fall of the tower of Siloe (13, 14f).

It is in the same spirit that he has had recourse to new sources and, indeed, the elements proper to Luke make up almost half of the work. These additions include especially the Infancy-narrative and the special Source-section, but they extend too to many elements in the Passion and Resurrection narrative. The Infancy-narrative enables the evangelist to begin the history of Christ with the annunciation of the birth of the Precursor. Indeed, his genealogy (3, 23-28) goes back much farther, to Adam, or, rather, to

God. The central Source-section is the treasury of St. Luke and there he has grouped, amid other riches, the loveliest parables in the gospels. And in the Passion and Resurrection narrative, as we have seen, the additions of the evangelist are of real importance. We have good reason to be grateful to St. Luke.

3. Language and Style of Luke

St. Luke has the best Greek style among the evangelists and that language is certainly his mother tongue. He often avoids the literary faults he finds in his sources; he chooses more exact Greek words and he usually suppresses foreign words and expressions. It is however true that he does not carry out these improvements consistently, and, not infrequently, he reproduces his sources just as he found them. This makes for an undeniable unevenness, in the style of the gospel, that is something of a mystery.

The evangelist was obviously very familiar with the Greek translation of the Bible (known as the Septuagint)—this, and not the Herbrew text, was read by most Jews outside of Palestine, and became the accepted version of the Christian Church. He has often sought to imitate the style of this Greek Bible, and with considerable success. Since he was conscious of writing a Sacred History which continued that of the Old Testament he tried to give it, as far as possible, the same coloring.

St. Luke has preserved traces of the Aramaic originals of his sources, but, as a rule, he avoids Aramaisms and translates Aramaic words, For example, instead of "Rabbi" Mark 9, 5; 10, 51) he has "Master" (9, 33) and "Lord" 18, 41); and instead of "Abba" (Mark 14, 36) he has "Father" (22, 42). In short, we may say that the style of St. Luke is complex. Left to himself it is excellent, but it is less good when he wishes to be faithful to his sources, and lastly, he can imitate, perfectly, the style of the Greek Old Testament.[8] The language and style of the gospel reveal a Christian who is familiar with the Old Testament books and an author who is familiar with the Greek literary style of his own time.

An interesting feature of St. Luke's style is his habit of

rounding off one subject before passing on to another; it is a characteristic that might easily lead to misinterpretation. When he says: "Mary remained with her about three months and then returned home" (1, 56), and goes on to tell of the birth of John, he does not mean to imply that Mary had departed before this event—he merely wanted to complete the episode of the Visitation before taking up another matter. In Chapter 3 he ends his account of the preaching of the Baptist by stating that Herod had John cast into prison (3, 19-20), and then immediately tells of the Baptism of Jesus (3, 21f); in other words, he finishes what he has to say about the ministry of John before going on to Jesus.

In quite the same way he indicates well in advance matters that will be dealt with later, and so ensures the unity of the narrative. In 1, 80 he mentions the sojourn of the Baptist in the desert, and later we learn that it was in the desert that the divine call came to him. (3, 2). At the close of the temptations the devil departed from Jesus "until the appointed time" (4, 13), that is to say, the hour of his arrest: "this is your hour and the power of darkness" (22, 53; cf. 22, 3). In 8, 2-3 we are told of the women who accompanied our Lord on his journeys, and these reappear, quite naturally, and with no need of any explanation of their presence, as those who prepare the spices and ointments for the body of Jesus (23, 55-56). We may also consider 3, 20 and 9, 9; 5, 33 and 11, 1; 9, 9 and 28, 8; 9, 10 and 10, 13; 9, 32 and 19, 38; 19, 27 and 21, 23-24.

If the style of the third gospel is complex, it is, in great measure, because St. Luke is undoubtedly a poet. According to tradition he was an artist, and he is credited with the first painting of our Lady. It is rather easy to see how this legend could have grown out of the word-picture he has drawn of her in his Infancy-narrative. And surely it is because of its poetic depth that this same story has so inspired, indeed dominated, Christian art. Speaking still more broadly, we can scarcely realize how very different our picture of Christmas would be without these chapters. At the other end of the gospel we find the delightful story of the two disciples and the unknown Traveller on the road to

Emmaus, while in between there is so much beauty. We should be thankful to St. Luke not only for the treasures he has searched out for us and so carefully preserved, but also for the artistry that went into the setting of these many pearls of great price.

4. The Method of St. Luke

Our quick glance at the language and style of Luke is hardly enough to give us an adequate idea of his literary skill; we must look more closely at the gospel and examine certain passages in some detail. This is the most practical way—and the one that is likely to be the most profitable—of studying the method of St. Luke.

(1) THE LITERARY STRUCTURE OF LUKE 1-2

Luke's Infancy-narrative is composed in the form of a diptych and has two phases: before the births of John and Jesus (1, 5-26), and the account of the birth of both (1, 56-2, 52). Each of these phases has a complementary episode: the Visitation (1, 42-56) in the first case and the Finding (2, 41-53) in the second.[9]

1—Diptych of Annunciations
   1, 5-56

I. Annunciation of the Birth of John 1, 5-25.	II. Annunciation of the Birth of Jesus 1, 26-38
Introduction of the parents	Introduction of the parents
Apparition of the angel	Entry of the angel
Zachary troubled	Mary troubled
Fear not . . .	Fear not . . .
Annunciation of the birth	Annunciation of the birth
Q. How shall I know?	Q. How shall this be done?
A. *Reprimand* by the angel	A. *Revelation* by the angel
Constrained silence of Zachary	Spontaneous reply of Mary
Departure of Zachary	Departure of the angel.
	III. Complementary episode 1, 39-56.
	Visitation

Conclusion: Return of Mary.

2—Diptych of Births 1, 57-2, 52

IV. Birth of John 1, 57-58
Joy at the birth
with canticle element
(1, 58)
Circumcision and Manifestation of John 1, 59-79
Manifestation of the "Prophet"
Canticle: *Benedictus*

Conclusion:
Refrain of growth 1, 80

V. Birth of Jesus 2, 1-20
Joy at the birth
Canticle of angels and shepherds.

VI. Circumcision and Manifestation of Jesus 2, 21-35
Manifestation of the 'Savior'
Canticle: *Nunc Dimittis*.
Supplementary episode: Anna 36-38.

Conclusion:
Refrain of growth 2, 40.

VII. Complementary episode 2, 41-52.
The Finding in the Temple.
Refrain of growth 2, 52.

Even a glance at the plan of the Infancy-narrative, as it appears above in schematic form, brings home to one the intention of St. Luke. John the Baptist and Jesus are compared and contrasted, but the greatness of Jesus is emphasized even by the more developed account of his earthly origins. Within the parallel narratives the same point is made. Mary is clearly shown to be far superior to Zachary, and even more explicitly, the Son of Mary is placed on a pedestal and towers above the son of Zachary. For example, it is said of John that "he will turn many of the sons of Israel to the Lord their God" (1, 16), but of Jesus it is stated: "the Lord will give to him the throne of his father David, and he will reign over the house of Jacob forever; and of his kingdom there will be no end." (1, 32-33). The same contrast is maintained throughout the parallel narratives.

It is obvious that these two chapters have been very carefully composed and they offer a striking proof of St. Luke's

literary skill. Despite the artificial framework there is an air
of spontaneity about them, and the composition, though in
fact carefully studied, appears to be quite effortless; it is
this quality that separates art from anything less than art.

(2)—THE SERMON ON THE MOUNT IN LUKE[20]

Our Lord formulated the special character of the Kingdom of God in a discourse which Matthew (5-7) and Luke
(6, 20-49) have preserved in widely different versions. The
discourse in Matthew is much longer than that in Luke, but,
on the other hand, many of the pasages found in Matt. 5-7
occur elsewhere in Luke. It can be shown that St. Luke has
omitted, as being of little interest to his Gentile readers, all
that concerned Jewish law and custom, and, in general, we
may say that whereas St. Matthew, borrowing from other
discourses of our Lord, has added to the original Sermon,
St. Luke has omitted some of it.

We have seen that the original plan of the Sermon on
the Mount was along the following lines.[11] (The references
are to Matt).

Introduction: The beatitudes (5, 3-12).
Part I: Perfect justice
  General statement: perfect justice (5, 17.20).
  Five concrete examples: (5, 21-24. 27-28. 33-37. 38-42.
    43-48).
Part II: Good works
  General statement: (6, 1).
  Three concrete examples (6, 2-4. 5-6. 16-18).
Part III: Three warnings
  (a) Do not judge (7, 1-2).
      Example: Parable of the mote and the beam (3-5).
  (b) Beware of false prophets (7, 15).
      Example: Parable of the tree and its fruits (16-20).
  (c) Practice justice (7, 21).
      Example: Parable of the two houses (24-27).

In his gospel St. Matthew has made considerable additions to the original Sermon, while St. Luke has done
quite the opposite and has omitted much of it. He sets
aside the section regarding our Lord's attitude to the Law
(Matt. 5, 17-48) and the passage concerning the Jewish

works of piety—this is perfectly in accordance with his method of adapting the gospel for his Gentile readers.

In Luke the discourse is introduced by the beatitudes and woes (20b-26). Only a very small part of the matter dealt with in the antitheses (of the Sermon) is included—the recommendations of the fifth and sixth antitheses of Matthew;[13] but this is sufficient to prove that St. Luke had known the series of antitheses and had deliberately omitted all the rest. He has combined two sayings by introducing into the middle of the positive part of the sixth antithesis the corresponding part of the fifth:

Matt. 5, 43-48 = Luke 6, 27-28   Luke 6, 32-36
Matt. 5, 39-42 =   Luke 6, 29-30

Luke 6, 27-36 then becomes an instruction on the love of enemies. The whole section, beginning with the commandment "Love your enemies" (27a)—repeated in the conclusion (35a)—is a unit that is rounded off by v.36

Luke 6, 37-42 also forms a unit. The warning not to pass judgment on others, the parable of the mote and the beam, and the other elements, are all linked together. Here it is no longer a question of love of enemies (as in the foregoing passage) but of love of the brethren. The last part of the discourse (6, 43-49) regards the necessity of proving good dispositions in action, and the necessity of putting into effect the teaching one receives.

As a result of these changes, the plan of the discourse in Luke takes the following form:

Introduction: Beatitudes and Woes (20b-26).
Part I: Love of Enemies (27-36).
Part II: Fraternal Charity (37-42).
Conclusion: Necessity of Good Works (43-49).

It is, in the main, because of the omissions that the discourse of Luke has a different character from that of Matthew, but it is also true that the omissions were motivated by St. Luke's outlook and consequently by his editorial emphasis. In this way, the parable of the two trees (6, 43-44), instead of illustrating a warning against false prophets (Matt. 7, 15) has become a recommendation addressed to the disciples. Similarly, in Luke 6, 32-34 the reference to "publicans and pagans" is omitted (cf. Matt. 5, 46-47) and the conduct of Christians is opposed to that of "sinners" in general. In brief, St. Luke is concerned with the wider perspectives in Jesus' teaching, and detaches from it its Jewish background.

This lack of emphasis on opposition to traditional Judaism characterizes Luke's version of the Sermon. It shows how Luke's purpose is different from Matthew's when both report the original discourse. We can see that the original Sermon defined Christianity in terms of perfect righteousness and in terms of a religion that is more interior and purer than that of official Judaism. The additions which St. Matthew makes from other discourses of our Lord serve to underline the practical consequences of this teaching. St. Luke is concerned rather to emphasize the essential trait of that message—charity. It is around this theme of charity that the elements of the central section of Luke's discourse are grouped: the duty of loving one's enemies (27-36), the obligations of fraternal charity (37-42). It seems that St. Luke is far less interested in defining the spirit of Christianity than in pointing out the conduct which can give concrete expression to that spirit.

(3)—The Journey to Jerusalem 9, 51-19, 46

We have seen that the long section (9, 51-18, 14) has been inserted by St. Luke into the plan of Mark which he follows so closely. The sayings and narratives of this section are grouped together and the whole is fitted into the framework of a journey to Jerusalem, a journey which ends at 19, 46. On examination it can be perceived that this arrangement is artificial.

It is a striking fact, for instance, that, though these chapters are supposed to describe a journey from Galilee, all topographical references to any other place except Jerusalem are suppressed.[18] The journey is explicitly indicated in 9, 51: "As the time approached when he was to be taken up (i.e., out of this world) he set his face resolutely towards Jerusalem." The Samaritans would not receive him "because he was making for Jerusalem" (9, 53), and so he went on to "another village" (9, 56). In 10, 1 there is reference to "every town and place" where he was to go, and in 10, 38 while on his way he entered "a village." In 11, 1 he prayed "in a certain place." In short, we may say with Father Lagrange:[14] "In vain do we try to discover where he is; we know only that he is still in the land of Israel, because there is no indication that he has left it. Apart from references to Jerusalem there is no indication of place; the scene is always just 'somewhere.' "

In 13, 22 we are again reminded of the goal: "He went on his way through towns and villages, teaching and journeying towards Jerusalem." When he was warned to get away "from here" (13, 31) he replied: "I must be on my way today and tomorrow and the next day, for it cannot be that a prophet should perish away from Jerusalem" (13, 33)—and he apostrophied the city (13, 34-35). In 14, 25 we read that "great multitudes" accompanied him; it is like a solemn procession.

A reference in 17, 11 removes any doubt that the framework is artificial. Though he had begun his journey from Galilee in 9, 51, and had been on his way ever since, we are now told: "On his way to Jerusalem he was passing through the confines of Samaria and Galilee"—he is still at the starting-place! In 18, 31-33 he tells his Apostles plainly that this journey to Jerusalem is a journey to his death, and from now on the tempo speeds up remarkably, and other place-names appear, to mark the final stages of the journey.

He drew near to Jericho (18, 35) and entered the town (19, 1). This was near the holy city (19, 11) and he went on ahead of the others, "going up to Jerusalem" (19, 28). He drew near to Bethphage and Bethany (19, 28) and came to the Mount of Olives (19, 37). He wept over the city that now at last lay before him (19, 41) and, finally, he entered the Temple, his Father's house (19, 45-46).

The intention of the evangelist is manifest: to present dramatically the last journey of our Lord to Jerusalem. The over-all effect is striking, especially the mounting tension of the final chapters. But he has very obviously used this same journey to frame, and give a certain unity to, an

important collection of sayings and parables—it is significant that we have to be reminded (13, 22 and 17, 11) that
there is a journey at all. But this framework sets these
sayings of our Lord in relief and gives them an added
solemnity. And, all the while, the literary skill of St.
Luke is in evidence.

The plan of this long section is only one expression
among many of a constant preoccupation of the evangelist
—to center his whole gospel around Jerusalem, for Jerusalem is for him the holy city of God and the scene of
the sacrifice of Redemption. So he sets it at the center
of his gospel; for in Jerusalem the gospel begins (1, 5)
and in Jerusalem it ends (24, 52f). The Infancy-narrative
has two significant entries into the holy city (2, 22-38; 2,
41-50), and it is this same interest that explains why, unlike the natural climax of Matt. 4, 3-10, the culminating
temptation of our Lord in Luke is at the pinnacle of
the Temple (4, 9-12).

We have remarked that in the journey-passage the
mention of other place-names is omitted. Similarly, the
journey outside of Galilee (Mark 6, 45-8, 26) is not given,
and Caesarea-Philippi is not indicated as the place of
Peter's profession of faith. (9, 18-22). It is this fact too
that explains why Luke has no mention of any apparitions
of our Lord in Galilee. Christ had come to Jerusalem and
there had suffered and died and risen from the dead, and
it is from Jerusalem that he was to ascend, finally, into
heaven; a departure from the holy city would, in St.
Luke's plan, be an anti-climax. And, consistently, when
he came to write his second book (Acts), he took care to
show the Christian message radiating from the same
center: "You shall be my witnesses in Jerusalem and in
all Judea and in Samaria and to the ends of the earth"
(Acts 1, 8).

XII
Some Theological Ideas
of the Third Gospel

1. The Gospel of Mercy

Each of the gospels has its own characteristics, its own peculiar quality, and these depend, to a large extent, on the manner in which each evangelist presents the person of our Lord. For St. Luke, Jesus Christ is the Savior of men. He uses this title once only in his gospel, in the words of the angel to the shepherds: "This day has been born to you a Saviour." (2, 11). The title is not repeated, it is true, but it is significant that the evangelist has drawn special attention to the name given to the child at his circumcision—Jesus (2, 21). At any rate, the Christ of Luke is throughout, and before all else, a Savior who is full of compassion and tenderness and great forgiveness. And the gospel of Luke is a gospel of mercy.

St. Luke has a gentle soul; it is because of this that he sees so clearly the tenderness of Christ. It is characteristic of him that he has omitted the cursing of the fig tree (Mark 11, 12-14; Matt. 21, 18-19) and has given instead the parable of the barren fig tree (13, 6-9)—"let it alone this year also." In the same vein of tenderness and mercy he has assembled the three parables of Chapter 15: The Lost Sheep; The Lost Drachma; The Prodigal Son. St. Matthew, too, has the first of these parables, but the others are proper to St. Luke. We are told that God rejoices at the repentance of a sinner; we are shown the love of the divine Father for the prodigal child: "While he was still a long way off his father saw him and was filled with compassion. He ran and fell on his neck and kissed him tenderly." (14, 20). We too must have something of the mercy of a forgiving God and the father's gentle rebuke to the sulking elder son has a message for all of us: "It was fitting to make merry and to rejoice, for your brother here was dead and is alive, he was lost and is found" (15, 32).

Perhaps nowhere else as in the whole wonderful passage on the "woman of the city who was a sinner" (7, 36-50), do we see Christ as St. Luke saw him. The Lord does not hesitate between the self-righteous Pharisee and the repentant sinner, and his words are clear and to the point: "Her sins, her many sins, have been forgiven her, for she has loved much." (7, 47). St. Luke alone records the words of Jesus to the good thief (23, 43), and his prayer for his executioners: "Father, forgive them, for they do not know what they are doing" (23,34). He alone tells of the look that moved Peter so deeply: "And the Lord turned and looked at Peter intently" (22, 61). Everywhere, at all times, there is forgiveness. It has been well said: the gospel of Luke is the gospel of great pardons.

It is quite typical of St. Luke that in his gospel he has paid special attention to women, for in the world of his day the position of women was degraded; and this insistence of the third evangelist is all the more striking when we compare his gospel with Matthew and Mark. Among the women introduced by St. Luke are: Elizabeth, mother of John the Baptist (1, 39-58), Anna the prophetess (2, 36-38), the widow of Naim (7, 11-17), the repentant sinner[1] (7, 36-50), the women of Galilee who accompanied Jesus on the public ministry, notably Mary Magdalen, Joanna and Susanna (8, 2-3), the sisters of Bethany, Martha and Mary: "Martha, Martha you are anxious and troubled about many things, while few things are necessary, or only one. Mary has chosen the better part which shall not be taken from her" (10, 41-42). There are, too, the woman who proclaimed the mother of Jesus blessed (11,

27-28) and the women of Jerusalem who encountered Christ on his way to Calvary (23, 27-31). We find, besides, two parables proper to Luke in which women figure: the Lost Drachma (15, 8-10) and the Unjust Judge (18, 1-8).

Finally, it is impossible not to recognize that the person of our Lady is shown in vivid light in the Infancy-narrative. God deigns to inform her of the great thing he is to do in her, and the lingering echo of the angel's "full of grace" is heard before-hand in the *Magnificat*. "Already her maternal brow shines with the promised halo that shall be hers owing to the salutation with which all generations are to greet her in their prayers. That prediction of her blessedness has indeed been fulfilled by all generations who have saluted her as Mother of God."[2]

The gentle heart of St. Luke beats for the distressed, the poor, the humble. His sensitive soul perceived the tenderness of Christ. His gospel of mercy and pardon is the gospel of the supreme Physician of souls who has told us that "the Son of Man has come to seek out and save the lost" (19, 10). And if the Lord at his birth was hailed as Savior (2, 11) it is also true that the last message of Christ to his disciples is a message of repentance and forgiveness: "Thus it is written, that Christ should suffer and should rise from the dead on the third day; and that in his Name repentance, in view of the forgiveness of sins, should be preached to all nations." (24, 46-47).

The message of the third gospel and its purpose have been strikingly expressed by Father Lagrange:[3] "In reading this gospel of mercy and of repentance, of total renunciation motivated by love; in considering these miracles inspired by goodness, this understanding of sin which is not complacency but which brings with it the divine gift of sanctification; in learning to know how a most pure Virgin and most tender Mother had given birth to the Son of God, and how he had consented to suffer in order to lead men to the Father—in all this the noble Theophilus would perceive the reason for that moral transformation which had taken place before his eyes, and which had doubtless begun in his own heart, and he would have

judged this reason good and solid: the world had found
a Savior."

2. The Holy Spirit

Jesus as the Messiah is the bearer of the Holy Spirit—
this is a truth emphasized by St. Luke.[4] After the baptism
and temptation it is "in the power of the Spirit" that
Jesus returned to Galilee and began his Messianic work
(4, 14), and his very first words were a quotation of Isa.
61, 1f: "The Spirit of the Lord is upon me because he has
anointed me to preach the good news to the poor" (Luke
4, 18). The whole public ministry is thus put under the sign
of the Spirit and all the works and teaching of Christ must
be seen in the light of this introduction.

In the early part of his gospel St. Luke has named the
Holy Spirit very often, but in the later chapters such references are much rarer; yet there are a number of significant
texts. In 10, 21 Christ "rejoiced in the Holy Spirit" at the
manifestation of his Messiahship to the unworldly. The
Holy Spirit is, in the estimation of Jesus, the "good thing"
par excellence (11, 13). Finally, the Risen Christ guaran-
teed that he would send the "promise of the Father," the
"Power from on high," upon his disciples (24, 49; cf
Acts 1, 8), for the Holy Spirit is the gift of the Risen and
Ascended Lord (John 7, 38f; 14, 26).

In Luke 1-2 almost all the characters are said to be
moved by or filled with the Holy Spirit: John the Baptist
from his mother's womb (1, 15.80), his parents Zachary
(1, 67ff) and Elizabeth (1, 41ff), as well as Simeon (2,
27ff) and Anna (2, 36). In all these cases the Holy
Spirit is the spirit of prophecy, and throughout Luke the
Holy Spirit is presented as a supernatural divine power.
Perhaps the clearest text is 1, 35 where our Lady is told.:

The Holy Spirit will come upon you, and

the Power of the Most High will overshadow you.
Here we have parallelism, that is, each member of the
verse says the same thing in different words; it follows
that Holy Spirit = Power of the Most High.

In other words, St. Luke shows us the activity of the
Holy Spirit rather than the divine Person himself, and the

same is true in Matthew and Mark. St. John, however, tells us that the Spirit is a Paraclete, an Advocate, just like the Son (14, 16) and, indeed, it is clear throughout the discourses after the Last Supper that the Holy Spirit is a Person, sent by the Father and the Son. But this more developed doctrine of the Trinity is not elaborated in Luke.

3. Prayer

Luke is the gospel of prayer, and the supreme example of prayer is given by Jesus Christ himself.[5] This essential fact is not neglected by Matthew and Mark. According to the three Synoptics Christ prayed in Gethsemani; he prayed after the first multiplication of loaves (Mark 6, 46; Matt. 14, 23); he prayed in Capharnaum after he had cured many (Mark 1, 35).

But St. Luke speaks of the prayer of Christ in eight further circumstances. He prayed at the Baptism (3, 21), he retired into the desert to pray (5, 16) and before choosing his Apostles he spent the whole night in prayer (6, 12). He prayed before the confession of Peter (9, 18) and later he told Peter that he had prayed specially for him (22, 32). He prayed at the Transfiguration, and it was the sight of him in prayer that moved his disciples to ask to be taught how to pray (11, 1). He prayed on the Cross for his executioners (23, 34). Indeed, we might add that the surrender of his soul to God was a prayer (23, 46).

Our Lord often recommended prayer to his disciples: persevering prayer like that of the importunate friend (11, 5-13) or of the widow before the unjust judge (18, 1-8). They must pray to obtain the Holy Spirit (11, 13) and, in short, they ought to pray at all times (21, 36). Their prayer must be true prayer, like that of the publican (18, 13).

Prayer is necessary for all men, for the individual Christian, but it is the special office of the Church to give glory to God. It is, perhaps, not always recognized that the third gospel has furnished the Church with her canticles of praise: the *Benedictus* at Lauds, the *Magnificat* at Vespers, the *Nunc Dimittis* at Compline, and the theme of *Gloria in Excelsis* in the Mass. But it is not surprising to

find these canticles in Luke, for the whole of the gospel
sheds an atmosphere of joy and peace.

Joy is mentioned at the birth of John (1, 14.58), at the
annunciation to Mary (1, 28), at the visitation (1, 41.44)
and at the angel's message to the shepherds (2, 10). The
seventy-two disciples returned rejoicing from their mission,
and Jesus pointed out to them the true motive of joy
(10, 20), and he himself "rejoiced in the Holy Spirit"
(10, 21). The crowds rejoiced at the works they witnessed
(3, 17); Zacheus received Jesus joyfully (19, 6). The
disciples rejoiced on the occasion of the entry into Jerusalem (19, 37) and after the Ascension they returned to
the city with great joy and praised God in the Temple
(25, 52). The parables of Chapter 15 depict the joy of
God himself at the repentance of a sinner.

Peace follows on this joy, the peace which Jesus gives
(7, 50; 8, 48), the peace that came into the world with
his coming (2, 14.29). It is this same peace that the Risen
Christ gave (24, 36). But peace and joy are the fruits
of prayer, of close personal union with Jesus Christ the
Savior.

4. The Influence of St. Paul

It is quite certain that St. Luke was a disciple of St. Paul,
and the influence of Paul can indeed be traced in the
third gospel. This is not so much a matter of vocabulary—
though there are resemblances—or of traditions—though
in the account of the institution of the Eucharist (Luke 22,
19f; I Cor. 11, 24f) both follow a similar tradition—as
of a common atmosphere of thought and sentiment. Both,
for example, insist on the theme of the universality of
salvation (Luke 2, 30f; 3, 23, 38; 13, 28f; 14, 23; 24, 46f;
Rom. 1, 16; I Tim. 2, 4; Tit. 2, 11). This is not to say that
the other Synoptics do not make it clear that salvation is
offered to all men (and not to the Jews only), but that this is
more emphatically the view of St. Luke.

The atmosphere of joy that we have noted in Luke is
like that of the Pauline epistles. In both we find frequent
invitations to serve the Lord in thanksgiving and joy (Luke
5, 25f; 10, 17; 18, 43; 19, 37; 24, 52f; Phil. 4, 4; I Thess.

5, 16; Rom. 12, 12 etc.). In both we find the same press-ing exhortation, by word and example, to have recourse to prayer (Luke 3, 21; 5, 16; 6, 12; 9, 18.28f; 11, 1-13; 18, 1-5. 9-14; 22, 32; 33, 34.46; I Thess, 5, 17; Col. 4, 2; Eph. 6, 18; Phil. 1, 3-6; etc.), and the same manner of indicating the action of the Holy Spirit on the conduct of life (Luke 3, 16.22; 4, 1.14.18; 10, 21; 11, 13; 12, 10.12; 24, 49; Gal. 3. 2-5.13f; 5.22; I Cor. 6, 11; 12, 13; II Thess. 2, 13; Rom. 8, 2.9; 14, 17; etc.).

St. Luke, alone among the Synoptics, gives Christ the title "Lord": 7, 13.19; 10, 1.39.41; 11, 39; 12, 42; 13, 15; 16, 8; 17, 5f; 18, 6; 22, 61; 24, 3.34. In the Greek trans-lation of the Old Testament Yahweh was rendered *Kyrios* (*"Lord"*), and the early Christians, from the first, gave this same divine title to Christ. "Lord," for us, has lost its very specific meaning, but the quite definite signification it had in the primitive Church is brought out by such texts as these: "If you confess with your lips that Jesus is the Lord . . . you will be saved" (Rom 10, 9), and "every tongue must confess that Jesus Christ is Lord" (Phil. 2, 11) —in both cases the divinity of Christ is professed. And when St. Luke uses the title he is writing as a Christian firm in his faith and so applies this Christian title to the Savior—for Jesus was not addressed as "Lord," in this full sense, during his lifetime.

It is not necessarily the influence of Paul only that has moved the evangelist to use the title "Lord" so frequently, for many of the concepts in the epistles go back beyond Paul to the primitive tradition. Such are the divine Son-ship of Christ, the universality of salvation and the im-portance of faith as a condition of entry into the King-dom of God. It is precisely these ideas that we find in Luke, and not as part of the preaching of the Apostle, but as they figured in his own written sources. Doubtless, in reproducing these concepts, he was influenced by the teaching and the expressions of his master. But despite his origin and his education, despite his close contact with Paul, despite the Gentile-Christian readers to whom his gospel is addressed, St. Luke reproduced, substantially, the primitive catechesis, the tradition of the apostolic Church.

XIII
Authorship of
the Fourth Gospel

The problem of the authorship of the fourth gospel is very involved, particularly because even the traditional evidence is not quite unanimous. However, the weight of tradition is unquestionably in favor of attributing the gospel to St. John the Apostle, and, despite sustained criticism of this view in recent times, it has not, by any means, been disproved. Indeed, when all the aspects of the case are taken into account, Johannine authorship, in some shape or form, would seem to be demanded.

1. Testimony of Tradition

According to the main stream of early Church tradition, John the Apostle, the son of Zebedee and brother of James, wrote, in old age, the fourth gospel, at Ephesus. The principal witness of this tradition is Irenaeus.

Irenaeus in his *Adversus Haereses* (c. 180) writes:

> Afterwards (i.e., after the other gospels had appeared) John, the disciple of the Lord, who also reclined on his breast, published his gospel while staying at Ephesus in Asia.

He also says that John lived in Asia until the reign of Trajan (98-117). The testimony of Irenaeus gains in weight when one remembers that, according to himself, he had, in his youth, known Polycarp bishop of Smyrna, and that the latter had known John personally.

Other witnesses are:

Polycrates of Ephesus, in a letter to Pope Victor (*c.* 190) mentions John who was both a witness and a teacher, who leaned upon the breast of the Lord, and being a priest wore the *petalon* (priestly insignia): "he also sleeps at Ephesus."

Clement of Alexandria (=*c.* 211-216) says that after the death of Domitian (81-96) John returned to Ephesus, from the island of Patmos. Elsewhere Clement states:

> Seeing that other gospels set forth only the material story, John, the last of all, entreated by his familiar friends and divinely upheld by the Spirit, wrote the spiritual gospel.

The Anti-Marcionite Prologue (160-180):

> The gospel of John was revealed and given to the churches by John, while still in the body, as one Papias of Hierapolis, a dear disciple of John, recorded in his last five books.

The Muratorian Canon (180-200):

> The fourth gospel is that of John, one of the disciples.

But there were also some in the early Church who would not accept this tradition. Irenaeus testifies that it was rejected by some anti-Montanists, and, according to Eusebius, it was discounted by the Roman priest, Gaius. From Epiphanius of Salamis we learn that it was opposed by an heretical sect called the Alogi. However, this opposition was confined, and soon disappeared altogether, and from the beginning of the third century the apostolic origin of the fourth gospel was universally accepted.

In the nineteenth century, however, the tradition was again questioned and ever since many scholars have denied that the Apostle was the author of the gospel. They at-

tribute it to a certain "John the Presbyter" or claim that
the writer of it is quite unknown. They question the traditional evidence on the following grounds:

(1) The John mentioned by Polycrates and Irenaeus is
not the Apostle, but a "presbyter" of the same name, who
was also an eyewitness and a disciple of the Lord. The
weight of the testimony of Irenaeus rests on the authority
of Polycarp, but neither an extant *Life* of Polycarp nor
his epistle to the Philippians mention his close connection
with the Apostle; the omission of any reference to St.
John in the letter is all the more surprising because St.
Paul is eulogized in it. It appears, then, that the John whom
Polycarp had known was not the Apostle, and Irenaeus was
mistaken in thinking that he was. This is all the more
likely since Irenaeus is certainly in error when he makes
Papias a hearer of the Apostle John. In this he is cor-
rected by Eusebius who points out that Papias, in his
prologue, makes it quite clear that he was no eyewitness
or hearer of the Apostles.

Besides, Papias himself names a "John the Presbyter" or
Elder, who is certainly not the Apostle. He writes:

> If, then, anyone came who had been a follower of the
> elders, I enquired into the sayings of the elders—
> what Andrew or what Peter *said,* or what Philip or
> Thomas or James or John or Matthew or any of the
> disciples of the Lord *said*—and the things which
> Aristion and the Elder John, the disciples of the
> Lord, *were saying.* For I did not think that what was
> to be had from books would profit me as much as
> what came from the living and abiding voice.

It should be noted that this whole argument at most sug-
gests the *possibility* that Irenaeus and Polycrates may have
confused a disciple of the Lord, named John, with the apostle
of the same name. Besides, though Irenaeus has erred with
regard to Papias the the case is surely different when he gives
his own reminiscences.

(2) Another objection raised is that John the Apostle
never went to Ephesus but died a martyr's death in Pales-

tine, either in 44, with his brother James, or later, between 64 and 70.

(i) Mark 10, 39. This is, apparently, a prophecy that the sons of Zebedee would share the suffering of their Lord, and, probably, that they should be martyred; it would not have been recorded had it not been fulfilled by the time Mark was written.

But, in fact, Mark 10, 38 f., is not necessarily a prophecy of a violent death, and even if it is so interpreted there is no reason why St. Mark should not have recorded it even though, as regards one of the brothers, the prophecy had not yet been fulfilled.

(ii) An epitomist of the historian Philip of Side (430) gives the following quotation: "Papias, in his recent book, says that John the Theologian, and James his brother, were martyred by the Jews."

(iii) The monk Georgios Hamartolos (ninth century) gives a similar reference to Papias: "Papias, who was an eyewitness of him (John), in the second book of the Sayings of the Lord, says that he was killed by the Jews."

(iv) Two martyrologies (liturgical calendars giving the names of martyrs and the date of their martyrdom) suggest that James and John suffered a similar fate, apparently at the same time:

A Syrian martyrology, drawn-up at Edessa *c.* 411, commemorates, on December 27, "John and James the Apostles, in Jerusalem."

The Calendar of Carthage (*c.* 505) contains two references to John the Baptist, one of which must certainly be a mistake for John the Apostle. Probably the error is in the entry under December 27: "Commemoration of St. John the Baptist and of James the Apostle whom Herod slew."

What is the value of these arguments? We may surely accept, as obviously unbiased, the judgment of a modern scholar who, while not accepting the tradition of Johannine authorship, nevertheless discounts the evidence of the sources just indicated.[1] "It is impossible to feel confidence in the witness of the epitomist of Philip and of George to the text of Papias. Neither was an accurate historian. . . .

The martyrologies can hardly stand as independent witnesses. . . . It is true that the tradition of John's martyrdom solves some problems; but it is not the only possible solution, and in any case we cannot martyr the apostle for our convenience in handling critical problems. The martyrdom tradition may have arisen simply on the basis of Mark 10, 39."

(3) Also to be noted is the silence of some who would have been expected to have known of the stay of St. John at Ephesus. On this ground it is held that the statement of Irenaeus to the effect that Polycarp had known John seems to be erroneous. A *Life* of Polycarp is extant, and it says nothing of the relation between him and John, and Polycarp shows no knowledge of the fourth gospel.

However, this last point, at least, can be contested. The letter of Polycarp to the Philippians has a citation that is a fusion of two texts found in the epistles of St. John (1, John 4, 2-3 and 2 John 7), and the citation expresses one of the major themes of the fourth gospel: the coming of Jesus Christ in the flesh.[2]

Ignatius, bishop of Antioch, was martyred in Rome in 115. In his letter to the Ephesians, written on his way to martyrdom, he emphasizes their close relationship with Paul but never refers to John—nor does he in any other epistle.

But this objection is not as serious as it appears because, in the context, it is easy to understand that Ignatius was preoccupied with St. Paul, and, more especially, with the latter's journey to Rome which led, ultimately, to martyrdom. With the prospect of a violent death in sight, Ignatius had no occasion to recall St. John who had died peacefully at Ephesus, at an advanced age, some years previously.

Conclusion

It would appear that the traditional attribution of the fourth gospel to St. John the Apostle, and the tradition of its composition in Ephesus, are by no means unassailable. But, at the same time, it is clear that the tradition which attributes the gospel to St. John is still in possession; it may have been questioned, but it has not been disproved. It should be noted, moreover, that even if the tradition of an early martyrdom of the Apostle is accepted, the gospel can still be attributed to St. John. Many eminent scholars believe in the existence of a "Johannine school"—a group of disciples of the Apostle. In this view, the gospel is substantially the work of St. John, but its present form may be due to the disciples who published it after the death of their master.[3] This theory does, at least, safeguard the Johannine origin of the gospel.

2. New Testament Witness to St. John

Since it seems reasonable that the Johannine authorship of the fourth gospel should be accepted, we may see, briefly, what the New Testament has to tell us about the Apostle.[4]

John and James form the second pair of brothers called by Jesus to be his Apostles (Mark 1, 19f.). Their father was named Zebedee (Mark 1, 20) and their mother was Salome (Mark 15, 40; Matt. 27, 56). Like their father, the "sons of Zebedee"—as they are frequently called in the gospels (e.g., Mark 10, 35; Matt. 20, 20)—were fishermen on the lake of Gennesareth. Because of their impulsive temperament Jesus called them "sons of thunder" (Mark 3, 17; Luke 9, 54). With Peter they formed the inner circle of the three privileged disciples (Mark 5, 37; 9, 2; 14, 33). They wished to receive the places of honor in the Kingdom (Mark 10, 33). John is named alone in Mark 9, 38 and Luke 9, 49. In Acts he stands next to Peter (1, 13; 3, 1 f.; 4, 13.19; 8, 14). In Gal. 2, 9 Paul designates him as one of the "pillars" of the early Church. There is no further mention of him in the New Testament, apart from Apoc. 1, 1.4.9; 22, 8—though some would deny that the John named is the Apostle.

The fourth gospel does not name its author, or, at least, not directly. In the Appendix (Ch. 21)—probably not written by the author of the gospel—the "disciple whom Jesus loved" (21, 20-33) is introduced as a trustworthy authority for the content of the gospel, and, indeed, as its author (21, 24.) Who is this "beloved disciple"? At the Last Supper he lay on the breast of Jesus (13, 23). At the foot of the Cross the Mother of Jesus was confided to his care (19, 26). On Easter Sunday he went with Peter to the sepulcher and believed in the resurrection (20, 3). At the lake of Tiberias he recognized the Lord sooner than the other disciples and heard from him a mysterious prophecy (21, 7.20-23). In two other places an unnamed disciple appears—most probably it is the "beloved disciple" (1, 40; 18, 15 f.).

The "beloved disciple" is certainly an Apostle since, according to the Synoptics, only Apostles were present at the Last Supper. As "beloved disciple" he surely belongs to the privileged inner circle of Peter, James and John. He cannot be Peter—who is named with the beloved disciple (13, 23 f.; 2, 2 f.; 21, 20 f.). He cannot be James—who was martyred in 44 (Acts 12, 2), while the beloved disciple reached an advanced age, for this would seem to be the obvious meaning of 21, 20-23. John alone remains. It is noteworthy that neither James or John are mentioned by name in this gospel (except in the appendix 21, 2). All goes to support the view that the beloved disciple is St. John and so 21, 24 would indicate that the gospel was written by an Apostle.

3. Destination and Date

The fourth gospel is addressed to Christians—its purpose is to establish their faith on a sure foundation. But John has, too, a discernible polemical character, which serves to heighten the impression that it was, in fact, destined for Christian readers.

Opposition to Judaism is marked throughout this gospel, and, indeed, much of it is concerned with controversies between Jesus and the Jews.[5] "Jew" becomes a synonym for "unbelieving Jew" (cf. 2, 18.20.24; 5, 10.16.18; 6, 41.52 etc.). We are told that the Law came through Moses, but grace and truth through Christ (1, 17). Jesus brings to an end Jewish ritualism (2, 1-10) as well as the Temple and its cult (2, 13-22; 4, 21-23). Moses could not give the true bread from heaven, but this the Father did in sending his Son into the world (6, 32 f.). The Jews are not really Abraham's sons, but children of the devil (8, 39-44). The Scriptures, in which they hope to find life, bear witness to the Christ whom they reject (5, 39). This attitude of opposition to the Jews is not, of course, to be confused with any form of anti-Semitism, for the author of the gospel was certainly a Jew himself. It is reminiscent of St. Paul's outlook and is a witness to the sad, historical fact that "his own people received him not" (1, 11).

St. John also has in mind the false evaluation of John the Baptist by the "disciples of the Baptist." The existence of this group at Ephesus is proved by Acts 19, 1-8 and we know that some of them were still there in the third century. Therefore the fourth gospel is quite silent about the repentance preaching of the Baptist and presents him exclusively in the role of Precursor. He is not the light but bears witness to the light (1, 6-8); he is not the Messiah or Elias or the Prophet (1, 20 f.); he is only the friend of the bridegroom who must decrease while the bridegroom must increase (3, 28-30). His great glory is that he has recognized the Lamb of God (1, 29). This uniform presentation of the Baptist, so different from that of the Synoptics, is only understandable if he were, in certain quarters, taken to be the Messiah.

Where was the fourth gospel written? The Anti-Marcionite Prologue, Jerome and Epiphanius speak of its place of origin as Asia Minor. Irenaeus names Ephesus, and the Ephesian origin of the gospel is widely accepted, even by scholars who doubt that it was written by St. John.

The date of the composition of John cannot be fixed with certainty. According to Irenaeus and Clement of Alexandria, the Apostle lived until the time of Trajan (98-117) and so died about the year 100. In this case the gospel was written before the turn of the century, perhaps about 90—though parts of it may have been written earlier than that. The latest possible date has been determined by the Ryland's Papyrus. This fragment, which contains John 18, 31-33.37-38, was found in Egypt and is dated to the early part of the second century. If we allow time for the diffusion of John to Egypt, a date after 100 would appear to be ruled out. Thus, as far as our evidence goes, the decade 90-100 is a likely date for the composition of the fourth gospel, at least in its present form:

XIV
Literary Characteristics of the Fourth Gospel

1. Language and Style

The Greek style of the fourth gospel is highly individual and has no parallel in the New Testament, apart from the closely related Johannine epistles. It remains distinctive even in translation so that, if one is at all familiar with the gospels, one can straightway identify a passage from John. The language, though not literary Greek, is far from being merely popular, and the vocabulary, though remarkably limited, is adequate. One cannot really speak (as is sometimes done) of the poverty of St. John's language, because the style is deliberately repetitive, and the effect produced is one of solemn dignity.

The more one studies this gospel the more convinced one becomes that it is a work of genius. Yet it remains true that the over-all dramatic effect, which is so striking, appears to have been achieved without deliberate effort and without any studied technique. The art of the fourth gospel is, largely, unconscious art; the work seems to have grown spontaneously—one might say inevitably—out of the genius of the evangelist and the sublimity of his subject.

The style of St. John shows an undeniable Aramaic influence, but in tracing the extent of this influence critics are not agreed. Some scholars have argued that our present gospel was translated from an Aramaic original. An interesting supporting argument for this view is that some Greek Mss. of the gospel have variant readings which may very easily be explained as different translations of the same Aramaic expression.[1] However, the majority of scholars are not inclined to accept the Aramaic origin of John. It is held that the Aramaisms are too few to prove that the Greek was translated from an Aramaic original, and that they can be accounted for on the ground that the author of the gospel was accustomed to think and speak in Aramaic as well as in Greek.

The undoubted Semitic background to the gospel is of capital importance for the understanding of it, and it is essential to have in mind what we have said elsewhere about the Semitic way of thought.[2] Our manner of thought is abstract, a process of reasoning, and follows a direct line from principles to conclusion. We should realize that this is not the method of the fourth evangelist. St. John does not work with abstract concepts but with representations, with imagery that has something concrete about it.[3] Where we say: God is infinite perfection, St. John says: "God is light, in him there is no darkness" (1 John 1, 5). Where we say that Christ is the source of all grace—and the word "source" has ceased to be an image—Jesus says, in the fourth gospel: "I am the vine, you are the branches" (15, 5).

We tend to regard this last statement as a figure of speech; quite spontaneously (for this is our way of thinking) we interpret the declaration about the vine as meaning that the union of Christ with his own is *like* the union of branches with the vine. What St. John means is precisely the opposite! For him, the intimate union of vine and branches is only a *symbol* of the infinitely closer union of Jesus with his disciples. That is why Jesus can speak of himself as the *true* vine (15, 1)— the supreme truth that the vine symbolizes is fully realized only in him.

We must beware of misunderstanding these passages in which St. John's thought seems unquestionably to be contained in abstract expressions. Thus Pilate's question "What is truth?" is not at all the key to John 18, 37-38, for by taking the word in a philosophical sense he showed that he had not grasped what Christ meant. The truth to which Jesus has borne witness (18, 37) is no metaphysical abstraction, but religious truth, the revelation of God in his person, for, indeed, Jesus *is* Truth (14, 6).

Similarly, the expression "God is love" (1 John 4, 8) is not definition of God.[4] It is to be taken in just the same way as the declarations: "God is spirit" (John 4, 24) and "God is light" (1 John 1, 5), where St. John indicates an essential property of God. However, love is the most manifest divine attribute, the one that is most emphatically revealed, as is clear from 1 John 1, 9: God is love because "in this the love of God was manifested to us that God sent his only Son into the world so that we might live through him." This is the key to the interpretation of the sentence. John is not speculating about the nature of God, and the pronouncement "God is love" really means that God is the manifestation of love in so far as his self-revelation is motivated and characterized by love. His revelation and his love both find their perfect and concrete expression in Christ.

If our abstract modes of thought are absent from the fourth gospel, so also is our process of reasoning. St. John does not reason—he testifies, he affirms. He does not set out to prove a thesis by building up consecutive arguments until the conclusion is reached. Instead, his thought moves around a central point, a point that is no abstract idea, but Christ himself. He takes the various facets of this Reality one by one. He understands very well that human language is incapable of ever conveying the full meaning of Christ, still less of confining that plenitude within the limits of a formula. For him, then, Christ is light, life, truth. Each of these images stands for the whole Christ, and not just for any attribute of his, and so they are, in fact, interchangeable. Christ is Life, Christ is Truth, Christ is Light, he is each of these and he is all of them together.

We may illustrate this manner of thought by taking, in the discourse on the Bread of Life, the passage 6, 53-58. The Jews' question: "How can this man give us his flesh to eat?" (6, 52) cannot be fully answered at this stage in the gospel, but the response of Jesus (6, 53-58) is not just a mere repetition of the same idea. The thought moves around the reality: Christ, the Bread of Life. Already, in v. 51, this reality is set forth, and the objection of the Jews (v. 52) does not interrupt the movement of the thought. There is, in fact, a certain development, for the notion of life in v. 53 can be more clearly understood in the light of the teaching on the resurrection of the body (v. 54), and union with Christ (v. 56) is shown to be based on the union of Father and Son (v. 57). But all the time the central idea remains: Bread of Life.

In reading John we must, at every turn, come up against parallel situations. We should take care not to judge such passages by our standards, but we should rather strive to understand them in the same way that the first readers of the gospel did. This may not be easy for us, but if we keep in mind the points made above—St. John's imagery is concrete rather than abstract; his thought moves in concentric circles rather than in straight lines—we should be able to make the necessary readjustment.

2. The Unity of the Gospel

The construction of the fourth gospel is complex, a fact that will be readily apparent when we come to study its plan. In spite of a general impression of unity it is also true that, as one reads the gospel, certain indications of an apparent lack of unity are met with. The narrative does not always proceed evenly and sometimes a passage seems to be out of its proper setting. In order to rectify this seeming lack of cohesion many modern scholars have put forward theories of displacement; this is to say, they presume that, due to accidental circumstances, certain parts of the gospel are out of their proper context, and they rearrange the present order of the work so as to accommodate, in a more logical manner, these presumably displaced passages.

The proposed displacements which have won the greatest measure of agreement are as follows:[5]

(i) 3, 22-30 which seems to interrupt the Nicodemus discourse (3, 31 would appear to follow logically on 3, 21) should be placed between 2, 12 and 2, 13. This change would improve the itinerary since Jesus, in Galilee in 2, 1-12, next comes into Judea (3, 22) before going to Jerusalem (2, 13).

(ii) Chapter 6 should stand between chapters 4 and 5. Again the itinerary is improved. As the gospel stands Jesus is in Galilee (4, 54), goes up to Jerusalem (5, 1), crosses the sea of Galilee (6, 1)—no mention being made of his return from Jerusalem—and moves about in Galilee since he is unable to move freely in Judea (7, 1). If Ch. 6 is taken before Ch. 5 the course of events is as follows: Jesus is in Galilee (4, 54), crosses the lake (6, 1), goes up to Jerusalem (5, 1) and returns to Galilee (7, 1).

(iii) 7, 15-24 should be read after 5, 47 for the passage continues the argument of Ch. 5 and interrupts the natural connection between 7, 14 and 7, 25.

(iv) 10, 19-29 should be read after 9, 41. The "division" of 10, 19 follows naturally on the miracle of Ch. 9, and so does the remark of 10, 21; 10, 18 is admirably taken up by 10, 30.

(v) Chapters 15 and 16 should be fitted in somewhere before 14, 31, which closes the farewell discourses.

A fatal argument against all such proposed changes is that there is no textual evidence in favor of any of them. All Mss. of John give the gospel in an order which—apart from insignificant details—is invariable; consequently any rearrangement cannot avoid being, in some degree, subjective. The exegete who seeks to rearrange certain passages which he has judged to be out of place in fact reshapes the gospel according to his way of thinking. If such manipulation of the gospel is admitted as a principal in the interpretation of John, very much will inevitably depend on the literary tastes and discernment of each interpreter. It is understandable that many outstanding scholars quite refuse to accept any of the proposed changes.

C. H. Dodd speaks for such scholars: "I conceive it to be the duty of an interpreter at least to see what can be done with the document as it has come down to us before attempting to improve upon it. This is what I shall try to do. I shall assume as a provisional working hypothesis that the present order is not fortuitous, but deliberately devised by somebody—even if he were only a scribe doing his best—and that the person in question (whether the author or another) had some design in mind, and was not necessarily irresponsible or unintelligent. If the attempt to discover any intelligible thread of argument should fail, then we may be compelled to confess that we do not know how the work was originally intended to run. If on the other hand it should appear that the structure of the gospel as we have it has been shaped in most of its details by the ideas which seem to dominate the author's thought, then it would appear not improbable that we have his work before us substantially in the form which he designed."[6]

This is an eminently reasonable view, and any study of John should be undertaken in a like spirit; transpositions should be regarded as a last resort. In this matter it would be well to recall what has been said about the author's manner of thought. Since the composition of the book has not been governed by our concept of logical sequence it should not surprise us if at some points the development, to our way of thinking, appeared strained. It will be noted, too, that many of the emendations have been suggested on the ground of improving the order of the journeys of Jesus; but this is a criterion that has little weight in a gospel whose movement is dictated by theological rather than by chronological and topographical considerations. On the whole, it is best to regard the fourth gospel as a deliberately planned writing, the work of an author of genius, while at the same time one recognizes that it cannot altogether be measured by our western standards of logical thought and literary style.

Note: The Problem of Certain Passages

Our position on the over-all unity of the gospel does admit of exception. There are a few passages which, on weighty literary or textual grounds, can be shown to fall outside the main gospel plan.

(1) Chapter 21

Quite clearly, the gospel ends at 20, 30-31—Chapter 21

is an *appendix*. This is the view held by almost all modern scholars. The position, as summed up by A. Wikenhauser,[7] is as follows:

Very probably, Chapter 21 was not written by the Apostle but composed by his disciples soon after his death —at any rate before the circulation of the gospel since it is present in all Mss. The arguments for this view are:

(*a*) The impression that 20, 30 f. is, and was meant to be, the conclusion of the gospel.

(*b*) Chapter 21 speaks of the death of the beloved disciple—this, at least, would be the natural interpretation of vv. 22-23.

(*c*) Only in this chapter is there mention of the "sons of Zebedee" (v. 2) whereas there seems to have been a deliberate effort to avoid naming them throughout the gospel.

(*d*) In language and style this chapter is clearly related to the rest of the gospel, yet there are so many differences that it can scarcely have come from the same hand.

The status of appendix does not, in any way, detract from the value or beauty of chapter 21 which remains an integral part of the gospel; but the recognition that is an appendix enables us to appreciate the natural climax of the gospel.

(2) The Woman Taken in Adultery 7, 53-8, 11

This passage is omitted by the very best early Mss., and indeed, the textual evidence in support of it is much less favorable than that for the Markan ending.[8] The passage is not in context in John, while in form and style it closely resembles the synoptic tradition, and is, indeed, quite like the style of Luke (a few Mss. have it after Luke 7, 36). It seems to have been inserted in John because of the reference to judgment according to the Law in 7, 51. Since it has been accepted by the Church as an integral part of Scripture, John 7, 58-8, 11, though not really part of the gospel of John, is most certainly inspired.

(3) 5, 3b-4

These verses are omitted by many important Mss. It is

now almost universally accepted that they constitute a gloss, or note added to the gospel (and not forming part of it) in order to explain the reference to the "troubling" of the water in v. 7.[9]

3. John and the Synoptics

The difference between John and the Synoptics, though more marked in the discourses, is not confined to these but extends also to the narrative, and indeed, to the whole plan and presentation of the gospel. This difference has been noted from the beginning—it scarcely could have been overlooked—and various theories have been put forward to explain it. The two extreme views are that St. John wished to supplement the other gospels and that he never really knew the Synoptics at all. The view of A. Wikenhauser, who strikes a mean between these two positions, is nearest the truth. He writes:[10] "Most exegetes acknowledge that John knew Mark, and admit the possibility of his knowing Matthew and Luke; but it is not at all certain that he did know all three Synoptics. . . . In fact it is very difficult, often indeed quite impossible, to fit the synoptic material with any certainty into the Johannine plan of the life of Jesus. If the fourth evangelist had had the intention of supplementing the Synoptics he would surely have taken care to harmonize his account with theirs. He presumes that the synoptic tradition is known to his readers, but he himself is quite independent of the other gospels."

This last point is of capital importance and neglect of it has too often hindered a more positive and rewarding approach to John. It has been far too easily taken for granted that the fourth evangelist, in writing his gospel, must have had the other gospels constantly in mind. Yet this view is obviously unreasonable. St. John (who, even if one does not admit that he is the author of the gospel in the strict sense, is certainly responsible for the tradition underlying it) was an eyewitness in his own right, and the actual author of the gospel (whether the Apostle or another) was patently a most original thinker and writer. We have seen, too,[11] that the framework of the Synoptic gospels is largely conventional and, especially, that the choice of material was quite selective. Besides, it is clear that St. Luke, as a result of personal research, has made important additions to the original plan.[12] Why then could St. John not have gone a step further and written his gospel quite independently of the Synoptic gospels? Surely an unbiased reading of his gospel will convince one that this is just what he has done.

It follows that John ought to be interpreted by itself and for itself, since even the aim of the fourth evangelist is different from that of the others. It was St. John's special interest to give theological depth to the portrait of Christ. While the Synoptic gospels tell of Jesus as he appeared to the eyes of his disciples during his ministry, St. John presents the picture of him that had taken shape before his own Spirit-enlightened gaze.

But if John is, essentially, independent of the Synoptic gospels, it does not, by any means, ignore the synoptic tradition. The main lines of the primitive gospel plan are found here also; the preaching of the Baptist, the ministry in Galilee, the last journey to Jerusalem and the Passion-narrative. There are, too, in the fourth gospel a number of sayings of Jesus quite like those in the Synoptics: 2, 19; 4, 44; 12, 25f.; 13, 16.20; 15, 20.

Yet these points of contact ultimately serve to emphasize the independence of St. John. Though he has followed the broad lines of the synoptic plan he has not felt himself bound by the convention which seemed to fit the ministry of Christ into one year and which indicated only one journey to Jerusalem,[13] for by his mention of three Paschs he shows that the ministry lasted more than two years and he tells us that Jesus visited Jerusalem frequently. And though he has shown that he knows how our Lord framed his teaching, he often chooses to give that teaching in his own words. In short, he follows his own plan and pursues his own purpose, knowing that his own presentation of Christ and his teaching cannot clash with any true portrait of him or with any authentic outline of his message[14]

XV

St. John
the Theologian

The fourth gospel is often characterized as the *theological* gospel and St. John is traditionally known as the *Theologian*. We should realize, however, that these terms are not to be understood in a modern technical sense, for the gospel is not a manual of systematic theology and the evangelist is not a dogmatic theologian. Theology, according to the original meaning of the word, is nothing else than knowledge of God and of divine things, and St. John is the Theologian, *par excellence,* because he has penetrated, more deeply than the other evangelists, the divine mystery of salvation; his gospel is theological because it reveals to us, more intimately, the meaning of Christ.

St. John's literary method and his style have been influenced by his own vision of Christ, and by his effort to share that experience with others. In the foregoing chapter we have considered only the material, merely technical, aspect of his style; now we have to see the deeper, and far more important, aspect that lies beneath the surface. It is only at this level that we can make contact with the real St. John, because, in a very true sense, this writer begins where all others, whether inspired or not, leave off.

1. Symbolism

The wide use of symbolism is an obvious characteristic of the fourth gospel. Such symbols are, for example, living water, bread of life, the vine, the good shepherd, but the method is best illustrated by a study of the term "sign" as used by the evangelist.

"Sign" (in Greek *semeion*) does not necessarily connote a miraculous event. Though on the four occasions when the evangelist refers to a particular action of Jesus as a sign (2, 11; 4, 54; 6, 14; 12, 18) such action is, in fact, miraculous, yet it is certain, in the context of the gospel, that other actions, where there is no miraculous element, are equally signs. This is true, for instance, of the clearing of the Temple (2, 13-25) and the washing of the disciples' feet (13, 1-20). We are obviously not meant to look for a deeper significance only in those actions that are expressly described as "signs"—the whole range of symbolism must be exploited.

Still, it is by contrasting "miracle" and "sign" that we can best understand St. John's intention. The restoring of sight to a blind man at Siloam (9, 1-12) is indeed a miracle, just like similar miracles in the other gospels (cf. Matt. 9, 27-31). The synoptists related such miracles for their own sake, or, at most, because they manifested the Messianic power of Jesus. But St. John is not interested in these miracles as such—his interest is in their symbolism, their signification. For him the giving of sight to a blind man is a sign of the spiritual light that Christ, who is Light, can give, because he viewed such actions of Jesus as visible pointers to a deeper, spiritual truth. Fortunately we are not always left to work out these hidden meanings by ourselves, for they are, in many cases, brought out in the discourse, that accompany the signs; we are also thereby provided with a criterion for judging others passages where such comment is lacking.

It may, perhaps, seem that the emphasis on the symbolism of gospel events would mean, or at least could mean, that these events are not historical. To put it bluntly, it may appear that St. John has contrived the events in view of the symbolism he wished to bring out. We have only to remember that the evangelist is intent on showing that Jesus of Nazareth—a real, historical Person—is the Messiah, the Son of God (20, 30-31); his argument would lose all its force if he were suspected of inventing the facts he relates.

Yet he has, undoubtedly, paid special attention to the symbolism of these facts, and, though he has by no means invented them, he has certainly *chosen* them, and that precisely because of their symbolism. For instance, in giving sight to the blind man, Christ is manifested as the Light of the world, and in the raising of Lazarus he is the Resurrection and the Life—so these two miracles find a place here. The symbolism of these facts is all the more striking because the facts are historical. We may, however, admit that the evangelist has modified details in order to emphasize the symbolism and so bring out the theological teaching that is his first concern.

2. Double Expressions

Another notable feature of John is the very frequent use of double or ambiguous expressions;[1] this practice involves a whole technique. Such expressions, when spoken by Jesus, are first understood by his interlocutors in the obvious or natural sense, and he then goes on to explain the deeper spiritual meaning. For example, in 2, 19, the Temple of which Jesus speaks is not the building—as the Jews believed—but, in reality, the temple of his body (2, 21).

More characteristic, however, are such words as the adverb *anōthen* (3, 3.7) which means "again"—and was so understood by Nicodemus—and also "from above"—the meaning really intended by Christ. The rendering of the adverb qualifies the meaning of "birth" (3, 3.7) and this is also misunderstood by Nicodemus. In 3, 14 we read of the Son of Man being "lifted up." The same expression occurs at 8, 28 and 12, 32 f., and in the latter case a note makes it clear that crucifixion is meant. The evangelist regards the "elevation" of Christ on the Cross as a symbol of his "elevation" to heaven by his Resurrection and Ascension. In St. John's eyes the Death, Resurrection and

Exaltation of Christ are all aspects of one and the same mystery, and so he can regard the exaltation on the Cross and the exaltation in glory as one movement.

The "living water" in 4, 10 signifies first of all running or spring water in contrast to stagnant water (and was so understood by the Samaritan woman); Jesus has used the expression in a spiritual sense, to signify a free gift of God. In 7, 38 f. it is further specified that "living water" symbolizes the Holy Spirit. Much the same is true of "living bread" in chapter 6. The starting-point is the theme of material bread given to the crowd. Then the line runs to the miraculous bread of the Old Testament, the manna, and its signification is further extended to take in the person of Christ and the eucharistic Bread. Other examples, where a word with a double signification is first taken in the more obvious or material sense, are the following: "to go" (7, 33-36), "servitude" (8, 33-36), "fallen asleep" and "to awaken" (11, 11-14). Even a whole sentence can be understood in two ways (11, 50).

In all these, and in similar cases, Jesus intends the full meaning from the beginning and it is only the interlocutors who misunderstand; this is an important observation. Even in such places as 3, 8 where there is a word-play on *pneuma,* meaning "wind" or "spirit" (so that the first part of the verse should read: "The wind blows where it wills") we cannot absolutely rule out the Vulgate rendering: "The Spirit breathes where he wills"; for St. John was aware of the ambiguity of the word.

In interpreting the fourth gospel we must be careful to give full weight to this technique of the evangelist. We should realize that he has chosen these expressions of Christ precisely because they have more than one signification, and that he clearly intends the two (or more) significations of each expression. We should not be true to his mind if we were to narrow his meaning to one or other alternative. Indeed, speaking generally, it would be unwise to feel that we had ever fully exhausted the meaning of any passage of this gospel.

If St. John uses ambiguous words it is not because he wants to be obscure, or wishes to hide something. Quite the opposite, in fact, because what he does is to look beyond the superficial signification of an expression to a deeper spiritual meaning. This method is to be understood in much the same way as his presentation of signs; not only the actions of Jesus, but his words too, are "signs." It is because they are words of Christ—"words of eternal life" (6, 68)—that they have a deeper meaning, and this truth can be effectively symbolized by the use of double expressions.

3. The Discourses of John

Nowhere does the difference between John and the Synoptic gospel strike one more forcefully than in the discourses of Jesus. In the first three gospels the langauge of our Lord, in his sayings and parables, is very much the same in each gospel; even where there is a notable difference in parallel passages it has to do with words and not with style. With John it is another matter. In the first place there are no developed parables here, and the allegories of the Good Shepherd and the True Vine are quite unlike anything in the Synoptics. The discourses of the fourth gospel are quite distinctive.

It is often urged that the differences can be explained on the ground of a change of audience: in the Synoptics Jesus was addressing the simple folk of Galilee, whereas in John his audience is composed of the cultured *élite* of Jerusalem. Like all *simpliste* solutions this argument is not even true to the facts. Even in the Synoptics we find accounts of controversies with the leaders of the people (cf. Matt. 21, 23-22, 46), yet these are not at all like the disputes of John (7, 14-8, 59). And on the other hand, the discourse in John 6, addressed mainly to Galileans, and the conversation with the Samaritan woman (Ch. 4) are as distinctly Johannine as any other passage in the gospel.

A very significant aspect of the problem is that the Baptist speaks in just the same way as Jesus (1, 29-31; 3, 27-30); and the style of the evangelist himself, in the prologue, and in the passages that are generally regarded as personal reflections of his (3, 14-21; 31-36; 12, 16-19), is no different. Most striking of all—the style of 1 John is remarkably close to that of the gospel. What, then, are we to say of the fourth gospel? The verdict, the only possible one, can scarcely be better expressed than in the clear, yet finely nuanced, conclusion of Dr. Grossouw.[2] "John treated his material very freely, particularly the words of Jesus, and this to such an extent that we must perhaps say that we can no longer call them literal. He has faithfully preserved their substance, but they have been completely recast. One may compare it to an old theme that has been reworked; to some classic motif that has been adapted by a modern writer. The transposition may have the appearance of a new work, but an experienced ear will detect the original theme immediately. This is true in a higher sense of the way in which St. John transmits the words of Jesus."

The evangelist himself has intimated that he has indeed interpreted the teaching of Christ. For instance, he remarks that a saying of Jesus was not fully understood until he had risen from the dead (2, 22), just like some of his signs (12, 16; 13, 7) and even the predictions of his resurrection (20, 9). St. John knows that the Spirit, whom Christ gave to his disciples, would remind them of his teaching (14, 26). But this was to be no mere recalling of the words of Jesus—he would lead them into "all the truth" (16, 13), that is, into the full meaning of the life and death and resurrection of the Lord, for the office of the Spirit is to render testimony to Christ (15, 26). It was with full confidence in these promises of his Master, and with the tranquil assurance that he was being guided by the Spirit of truth, that St. John wrote his gospel.

4. The Historical Character of the Fourth Gospel

In view of his predominantly theological interest, it is evident that it was not St. John's intention to write a work of scientific history. In fact, he handles his material rather freely and subjects it to his leading thought; he dominates his material—which is a very different matter from falsifying it in any way. He is interested in events and the meaning of events, but he is not unduly troubled with details, unless he finds some symbolism in them. The one fact that is of supreme importance for him is that Jesus of Nazareth, who really lived and died in Palestine, was the Son of God; or, to put it his own way, that the Word did in very truth become flesh and tabernacle among us.

If we are to keep St. John's approach to the gospel facts in proper perspective, it would be well to recall that the first three evangelists were in no way mesmerized by these facts. They did not feel that they had to give a verbatim account of the words and works of the Savior, for, when we compare these gospels it becomes at once apparent that St. Matthew and St. Luke especially permitted themselves considerable liberty in the presentation of the material. We are not, then, pleading for special treatment for the fourth evangelist; we merely stress the fact that by temperament and design he was more individualistic than the others, and more independent of the synoptic-type tradition.

The fourth gospel is essentially a theological work rather than a history, but it is presented in the literary form of a "gospel." A gospel is a recital of the historical narrative of the suffering, death and resurrection of Jesus Christ, prefaced by an account of his ministry. The aim of an evangelist is to set forth the knowledge of God contained in the Christian revelation; this revelation, as clearly in the fourth gospel as in the others, is an historical revelation. Consequently, it is of vital interest for the evangelist that what he relates did really happen, that he is dealing with *facts*.

But the evangelist is not debarred from interpreting the facts with which he deals, and when he does so he is not being unhistorical, for history, in any real sense, includes interpretation of the facts related. And as an evangelist, St. John, though not primarily an historian, is, nevertheless, dealing with history. The remark of P. Benoit is just as applicable to John as it is to the first Christian preachers. "The early Christians had not, perhaps, our regard for "history," but they had regard for the "historical." The preachers of the new faith did not intend to relate everything about Jesus, but they were careful to relate only what was solidly founded."[8] If St. John, by long reflection, was able to find a deeper significance in many actions of our

Lord he looked for that significance in solidly-founded facts. If his carefully-composed discourses brought out the more profound aspects of the teaching of Jesus, these discourses are founded on that teaching and are true to the mind of our Lord.

When we get down to details of chronology and topography we must never lose sight of St. John's essential independence of the Synoptics. We should not be perturbed by minor differences, nor even by apparent contradictions; there should be no question of smoothing out such differences by unjustifiable harmonization. For example, John has the clearing of the Temple at the beginning of the ministry (2, 13-21) while the Synoptics place it just before the last Pasch (Mark 11, 15-19; Matt. 21, 12-17; Luke 19, 45-48). It would be a puerile expedient to explain this discrepancy by supposing that the Temple was cleared twice over—for both John and the Synoptics quite obviously relate the same event.[4] Much more important are the points at which the two traditions meet, and by meeting emphasize the essential historicity of both. John and the Synoptics tell the same story; the main difference is that St. John the Theologian is less interested in the facts than in their symbolism.

XVI

Plan of
the Fourth Gospel

1. Plan of the Gospel

A. The Introduction   1.
   (1) The Prologue   1. 1-18.
   (2) The Testimony   1, 19-51

B. The Book of Signs   2-12,
  Section 1: Jesus is the Founder of a new religious
           economy, superior to the old 2, 1-4, 42.
   (i) Narrative: Miracle of Cana   2, 1-12.
  (ii) Narrative: Clearing of the Temple   2, 13-25.
 (iii) Dialogue: Rebirth   3, 1-21.
         Testimony of the Baptist   3, 22-36
 (iv) Dialogue: *(a)* Living Water   4, 1-15
             (b) True Worship   4, 16-26.
             (c) The Will of God   4, 27-38.
         Testimony   4, 39-42.

  Section 2: The Life-giving Word   4, 43-5, 47.
   (i) Narrative: Cure of a Nobleman's
         Son   4, 43-54.
  (ii) Narrative: The Sick Man at
         Bezatha   5, 1-18.
 (iii) Discourse: The Life-giving Word   5, 19-30
         Testimony of the Father to the Son 5, 31-47.

The plan given above takes for granted that the fourth evangelist is primarily interested not in chronology or topography but in *ideas,* consequently it aims at bringing out the theological development of the gospel. It is apparent that the significance of the plan cannot be appreciated at a cursory glance; indeed, a rather detailed explanation of it is called for. This is attempted in the following analysis.

2. Analysis of the Ideas of the Gospel

THE PROLOGUE (1, 1-18.)

The prologue introduces the fundamental themes (life, light, darkness, truth, witness, glory, the world) which will be subsequently developed. Since, however, it merely indicates these, it cannot be fully understood until the gospel as a whole has been read through. Some would see in the prologue a pre-existing Christian hymn which was taken over and used by the author of the gospel. If it is indeed a hymn—as it appears to be—it would surely be more reasonable, in view of its close relationship to the rest of the gospel, to attribute it, too, to St. John himself.

The concept of the "Word" figures prominently in the prologue. A sharp contrast is set up between this Word of God—who is Christ—and the Law (which is also God's word). It is affirmed that the Law did not, in any real sense, bring grace and truth; this is the work of Christ (1, 17). The Law is therefore, only a shadow of the true Word of God, the Word who "became man and pitched his tent among us" (1, 14). In the world but not recognized by the world, rejected by his own people, he yet grants the divine sonship to those who believe in him (1, 10-13).

THE TESTIMONY (1, 19-51).

Before embarking on his gospel proper, St. John brings forward a series of witnesses who bear testimony to the Messiah in a variety of Messianic titles. John the Baptist calls him the "Lamb of God" (1, 29-36) and the "Elect² of God" (1, 34). Andrew speaks of him as the "Messiah" (1, 41). For Philip he is "he who was spoken of by Moses in the Law, and by the prophets" (1-45), and Nathanael exclaims: "You are the Son of God; you are the king of Israel!" (1, 49). Jesus himself rounds off the list by adding his own special designation: Son of Man (1, 51).

The title used by the Baptist, "Lamb of God," is one that is variously interpreted. Many would argue that the Paschal lamb is meant. Some would see here a reference to the divinely-appointed leader of the people of God—God's flock—in much the same way that the lamb of Apocalypse is also a leader (7, 17). These identifications have much in their favor, and St. John most probably had them in mind, but they do not sufficiently explain the "taking away" of the sins of the world. Consequently, another explanation, which is gaining wide acceptance, is that "Lamb of God" stands for "Servant of Yahweh." In Isa. 53, 7 the suffering Servant was likened to a "lamb led to slaughter," and it is noteworthy that the Aramaic term *talya* can be translated "lamb" or "servant." The Baptist, then, points to the Lamb that is the Servant who suffers and dies for the sins of the world.

A further argument in favor of this interpretation is that another passage of Isaiah, which also treats of the Servant, lies behind the testimony of John.³ In Isa. 42, 1-2 we read:

> Behold my *Servant,* whom I uphold,
> My *Elect* in whom my soul delights;
> I have put my *Spirit upon him.*

In John 1, 29-34 this text is manifestly in mind: "Behold the Lamb (=*Servant*) of God" (1, 29); "This is the *Elect* of God" (1, 34); "I saw the *Spirit* descend and remain *on him*" (1, 32-33). It appears that here, too, as in the Synoptic gospels, these important texts of Isaias are very much to the fore.

The Book of Signs.
THE NEW BEGINNING.

The first episode or section of the gospel (2, 1-4, 42) may be regarded as an inauguration, a new beginning: Jesus the Messiah founds a new religious economy.

The miracle of Cana is solemnly described as the "beginning of signs" (2, 11) and, by that fact, we are sufficiently warned that we are not to take it merely at its face value. The water ("for the Jewish rites of purification"), turned into wine, symbolizes the old and imperfect order which yielded place to the new. In view of the author's interest in the sacraments, the wine of the Supper is also indicated. The narrative then turns to the clearing of the Temple, and there is an explicit reference to the perfect temple that will be constituted by the glorified body of the Savior (2, 21-22).

The meaning of these "signs" is brought out in the discourses. The dialogue with Nicodemus (3, 1-21) treats of a new birth. The phrase rendered "born anew" (3, 3.7) can, as we have seen, equally well mean "born from above" and, typically, St. John intends both meanings. True to the procedure of this gospel, Nicodemus understands the statement of Christ in a material sense (3, 4) and our Lord then explains that he means spiritual rebirth from above; his Baptism, which brings about this rebirth, is not in water only—as was the baptism of John—but in "water and the Spirit" (3, 5). Then follow an enigmatic reference to the death of Christ (3, 14-15) and a clear statement of the marvelous love of God (3, 16-18). Finally, the Baptist again bears witness to Christ and to the same great love (3, 22-36).

Baptism would still appear to be in mind in the discourse with the Samaritan woman (4, 1-15). The "living

water" (at first understood by the woman in the sense
of running water) which Christ gives, stands for the Spirit
(7, 39), and the rebirth of Baptism is in "water and the
Spirit" (3, 5). But there is a wider context, for the conversation with the woman now switches to the idea of
worship. The scene is highly dramatic, for the meeting
took place in the shadow of Mt. Garizim, and the woman
could point to the schismatic temple on top of "this
mountain" (4, 21). We now understand that the water
of the cistern dug by Jacob—like the water of Jewish
purification (2, 6)—will be replaced by the régime of the
Spirit; and worship, both on Garizim and in Jerusalem, will
give place to the new Christian worship (4, 21-24).

In the subsequent brief conversation with his disciples
our Lord summarizes his mission as a doing of the will of
his Father (4, 27-38). This is a truth that will be emphasized more and more as the gospel proceeds, and
the program traced here: "My food is to do the will of
him who sent me, and to accomplish his work" (4, 34),
will find its fulfilment only in his last words on the Cross:
"It is accomplished" (19, 30).

The woman had recognized Jesus as the Messiah (4, 29),
and the other Samaritans, who came to meet him and
hear his words, were convinced that here indeed was the
"Savior of the world" (4, 42). This faith and this acceptance should be viewed against the unbelieving attitude
of the "Jews" throughout the gospel.

THE LIFE-GIVING WORD (4, 43-5, 47).

Chapter 5 marks a turning-point in the fourth gospel.
Up to now (apart from the prologue, of course) the Messianic character of Jesus was in question, as well as the
superiority of the Christian economy over the old régime,
but henceforth it is rather the properly divine dignity
of Jesus that is stressed. At the same time, the opposition
that until now was latent, comes into the open, and becomes more and more pronounced.[4]

The suggestion, very often put forward, that Ch. 6
should come before Ch. 5 is, doubtless, attractive,[5] but,
apart from the fact that it has no support at all in any

of the Mss. of the gospel, the theological development would seem to demand the present order.[6] In Ch. 5 the reader is told of the identity, in will and work, of the Father and the Son, through the love of the Father and the perfect obedience of the Son; this teaching seems to prepare the way for the teaching of Ch. 6. Though it has been shown in Chs. 2 and 4 that Christ gives life, the way in which he does so is not considered until Ch. 6; for with the declaration: "I am the living bread" we learn for the first time that he himself is the gift which he brings (6, 35.48) and that the bread which he will give is his flesh for the life of the world (6, 51). But the life which Christ gives is that life which he eternally shares with his Father—a truth that is expressed in Ch. 5. We find, too, that certain verses of Ch. 6 (e.g., 38-40. 57a) echo the teaching of 5, 23-30, for when we examine the texts we see that the doctrine concerning life and resurrection is expressly propounded in Ch. 5, whereas in Ch. 6 the same ideas are subordinate to the main theme of that chapter, which is that Christ himself is the life-giving Bread.

The two narratives of this section—the cure of the Nobleman's son (4, 43-54) and of the sick man at the pool of Bezatha (5, 1-18)—have this in common that it is by his word that Christ effected the cures. He told the nobleman: "Go, your son will live," and the man believed in the *word* of Jesus (4, 50). In the other case he merely said to the infirm man: "Rise, take up your bed and walk"—and the man was cured (5, 8-9). That life-giving word restored to life the son who was on the point of death and the man who had been helpless for thirty-eight years.

The accompanying discourse (5, 19-30) explains why the word of Jesus is so efficacious: "As the Father raises the dead and gives them life, so the Son gives life to whom he wills" (5, 21). We now perceive that he can restore to life precisely because he *is* the life-giving Word. And if the Jews now accuse him of healing on the sabbath the day will come when it is Jesus who will pass judgment; for the Father has given him authority to execute judgment, because he is the Son of man (5, 27). Yet, Christ will not need to judge the unbelieving Jews—Moses himself will accuse them because they have not believed in the Scriptures which tell of Christ (4, 39-42).

THE BREAD OF LIFE (Ch. 6).

This section is composed after much the same pattern as the previous one: two miracles are followed by a discourse which explains the significance of the miracles. The narrative of the multiplication of loaves lends itself incontestably to a eucharistic interpretation. The account of the walking on the waters, which presents Jesus as being in some way beyond the laws of nature, is meant to clarify the close of the discourse (6, 60-71) where he replies to the difficulties of those who refused to accept his eucharistic doctrine.[7]

In the first part of the discourse (6, 22-34) Jesus points out the difference between a "miracle" and a "sight": the multitudes may have eaten the miraculous bread, but unless they realize its underlying signification it had no lasting effect for them. Just like the "living water" (4, 13 f.) the bread is "food of eternal life" (6, 27); and exactly as the Samaritan woman understood the words of Jesus in the most material sense (4. 15) so here the crowds take him up quite literally (6, 34).

Jesus corrects the misapprehension by pointing out that he himself is the bread of life (6, 35-50). Once again he is presented as the life-giver: "This is the will of my Father that everyone who sees the Son and believes in him should have eternal life" (6, 40); for he who believes in the Son of God has life here and now. But just as Jesus himself has come to do the will of his Father and is entirely subject to that will, it is also necessary that he who comes to Christ should be led to him by the Father: "No man can come to me unless he is drawn by the Father who sent me" (6, 44).

The teaching of Jesus becomes more emphatic still in 6, 51-58. It should be noted that the passage is welded into a unit by the phrase: "whoever eats this bread will live forever" occurring in vv. 51 and 58. This passage is the logical conclusion of the earlier parts of the discourse, for if Christ is both Bread and the Giver of bread, it follows that what he gives is himself, his own body and blood. The Jews ask: "How can this man give us his flesh to eat?" (6, 52); it is a question that is not answered at this stage, any more than the question of Nicodemus was answered: How can a man be born again (3, 4). These questions cannot be fully answered until the close of the gospel, but, at least, it is abundantly clear that the Eucharist is envisaged here, as Baptism was in Chapter 3.

The emphatic declaration of our Lord is undoubtedly a "hard saying" and as a result many of his disciples deserted him. Yet he had not left them entirely mystified but had given them a key to its meaning in a reference to the Ascension and in the significant opposition between the Spirit who vivifies and the flesh that is of no avail (6, 62-63). For it is by the Ascension that the body of Christ entered fully into that spiritual state when, penetrated by the Spirit, it can be given to the faithful in the Eucharist. Before Jesus was glorified the Spirit had not yet been given (7, 39), but after his Resurrection and his return to his Father he will possess even in his body the fullness of the Spirit which he will dispense by means of the sacraments.[8]

When the many disciples, scandalized by this teaching, had gone away, Jesus turned to the Twelve. This is John's parallel to the Synoptics' scene at Caesarea Philippi. Here, too, Peter is the spokesman and professes his faith in the Messiahship of his Master: "We have believed and we know that you are the Holy One of God" (6, 69). In the Synoptics the confession of Peter is followed by the first prediction of the Passion; here, too, the foretelling of the betrayal by Judas opens up the same perspective.

Chapters 7-12 really form a unit. The center of interest is Jerusalem; the leading ideas of light and life occur throughout these chapters and are always closely associated. The ground for the subdivisions we have made in this long section lies in the mounting opposition to Christ and the growing certainty that he is going to his death. At the same time, however, there is a corresponding development in his self-manifestation.

LIGHT AND LIFE OF THE WORLD (7-8).

The scene is set at the feast of Tabernacles to which Jesus had gone privately. Right at the outset we are told that his very presence was a cause of dissension and so the way is prepared for the series of controversies (7, 1-13). The discourse that follows is unlike any other in the gospel. All the others follow the usual Johannine pattern of dialogue rapidly yielding to monologue, but here it is dialogue right through. This makes for a mounting tension and there is a constant harping on hostile action against Christ: 7, 1.13.19.25.30.32.44; 8, 37.40.59.

It is, very probably, the setting at the feast of Tabernacles which has prompted a memorable saying of our Lord. During the seven days of the feast water was taken from the pool of Siloam and was solemnly carried to the Temple to be poured over the altar of holocausts. We are, doubtless, meant to have this in mind when we read that on the last day of the feast Jesus proclaimed:

> If anyone thirst, let him come to me,
> And let him drink who believes in me;
> As Scripture says: "Out of his heart shall flow streams
>   of living water" (7, 37-38).

This, and not the other, perhaps more frequent, reading (the difference is merely one of punctuation) gives the true sense, and Christ himself is indicated as the source of living water. The evangelist explains (v. 39) that this water symbolized the Spirit which, however, would not be given until Jesus had been "glorified," that is, had passed through death to his Resurrection and Exaltation.

The idea of judgment runs through this section and it is in this context that we can grasp the significance of the declaration of Jesus that he is the light of the world (8, 12). It is a feature of the fourth gospel, to be met with again and again, that Christ, by his very presence, causes division: men must be for or against the light, they cannot ignore it, for light shows up, light judges. But those who follow him will be guided surely, and in that Light will find life (8, 12).

The mounting opposition to Jesus means that the Passion is not far from sight and, again, he refers to it cryptically. He tells the Jews: "When you have lifted up the Son of Man, then you will know that I AM" (8, 28). The "lifting up" of the Son of Man was already mentioned in 3, 14—what is meant by it will be made clear in 12, 32 f. The "I am" is an echo of the divine name of Ex. 3, 14 (repeated in Isa. 43, 10.13); by applying that Name to himself Jesus claims to be divine. At the very end of the discourse he makes this claim again, and the reaction of his hearers is immediate. " 'Amen, Amen, I say to you, before Abraham was, I AM.' So they picked up stones to throw at him" (8, 58 f.). They understood very well what he meant and judged him guilty of blasphemy. This is the climax of the long series of conflicts, and it is evident now that the struggle will have issue in the death of Jesus.

JUDGMENT BY THE LIGHT (9-10).

This episode is highly dramatic. There is a very obvious contrast between the Jewish authorities—blind guides—and Jesus, the good shepherd.

We have seen that Christ can give life by his word because he is the life-giving Word; here he restores sight to a blind man because he is the Light of the world (9, 5). The restoring of sight is a typical Johannine "sign" of something much more profound. The deeper significance is hinted at by the evangelist's interpretation of Siloam as "Sent," for, throughout the gospel, Jesus is characterized as the one sent by the Father. It is clear that we are meant to look beyond the surface meaning of the miracle to the further meaning that lies beneath.

The cure took place on a sabbath and the Jews were immediately up in arms; the man whose sight had been restored was dragged before the Sanhedrin and was eventually excommunicated (9, 34). The drama of the situation is that, in his person, it is Christ who has been judged and

rejected. Ironically, however, it turns out that the judges
have, by their action, been judged; inexorably, the Light
has shown them up: "It is for judgment that I have come
into the world, that those who do not see may see and
that those who see may become blind" (9, 39).

The discourse on the Good Shepherd is to be understood against the background of *Ezechiel* 34. There the
rulers of Israel are condemned as false shepherds and God
declares: "I myself will be the shepherd of my sheep"
(34, 15). In John 10 the hirelings are the Jewish leaders
who have just cast out the sheep they should have
sheltered—but Jesus sought out the one who had been rejected; once again the judges are judged by their very
conduct. But John goes beyond Ezechiel, for this Shepherd
will lay down his life for his sheep (10, 11.15).

The epilogue (10, 22-39) centers on the Messianic
claims of Jesus. In 10, 24 he is urged by the Jews to tell
them plainly if he is the Messiah, and he does answer
them plainly: "I am the Son of God" (10, 36). In their
eyes he thereby was guilty of blasphemy, and an attempt
was made on his life (10, 33). It becomes more obvious
still that the Good Shepherd must indeed lay down his life.

VICTORY OF LIFE OVER DEATH (11, 1-53).

Instead of following the usual pattern of narrative leading to discourse, this section is formed of narrative + discourse. Jesus is in Transjordan when he is informed of the
illness of Lazarus and he does not depart from there
until he knows that Lazarus has died. Quite explicitly the
journey to Jerusalem is presented as a journey to death.
The disciples point out that the Jews had just tried to
stone him (11, 8) and Thomas says to the others: "Let
us also go, that we may die with him" (11, 16).

In the ensuing dialogue Martha at first believes that
Jesus is referring to the general resurrection (11, 23-24).
He gives her to understand that he himself is the resur-
rection, as he is life; he can give life and restore it at any
time. Martha's profession of faith in the Messiahship of
Jesus is exceptionally solemn: "I believe that you are the
Christ, the Son of God, who was to come into the world"

(11, 27). The miracle dramatizes the claim of Jesus: at his life-giving word the dead man rose up and came out of the tomb (11, 43-44).

The Jewish authorities reacted at once to the raising of Lazarus. Perturbed by the influence of Jesus and the compelling evidence of his "signs" (11, 47) they debated on what action should be taken. The high priest spoke: "It is expedient that one man should die for the people" (11, 50). This is a striking example of "Johannine irony." The advice of Caiaphas, if utterly unscrupulous, was sound political commonsense, but the evangelist is aware that the words had a deeper meaning of which Caiaphas himself was quite unaware. However unworthy, he was high priest, and as such had uttered a prophecy: "He prophesied that Jesus would die for the nation, and not for the nation alone, but to gather together the scattered children of God" (11, 51-52). This is an echo of chapter 10—the Good Shepherd must gather his sheep, even those not of the fold of Israel, so that there may be one flock and one shepherd (10, 16); but in order to do that he must lay down his life. Thus here, too, he is given over to death: "from that day on they plotted his death" (11, 53). By coming to raise Lazarus, Jesus had indeed come to his death; it is in view of his own self-sacrifice that he is manifested as Resurrection and Life.

LIFE THROUGH DEATH (12, 1-36).

Jesus has now been marked down for death by the Jewish authorities (11, 53) and the narrative of the anointing at Bethany follows with dramatic appropriateness. This anointing is explicitly associated with his burial by Christ himself (12, 7). Symbolically, then, we are to understand that he is already dead (11, 53) and buried (12, 7). In this context the triumphal entry into Jerusalem must have the signification of his triumph, his glorification (12, 12-15). The evangelist indicates that here is indeed a deeper meaning in these things when he notes: "At the time, his disciples did not understand this, but after Jesus had been glorified they remembered that this had been written

of him and had been done to him" (12, 16). On the occasion of the triumphal entry we meet with another example of Johannine irony. Annoyed by this popular
demonstration the Pharisees petulantly exclaimed: "the
whole world has gone after him" (12, 19)—this was true
to a degree that they did not suspect.

We have noticed that, in the gospel, there is a definite
movement towards a climax. It has become increasingly
apparent that a violent death is in store for Jesus and
in this last section the point is made quite explicitly.
The hour has now at last come for the Son of Man to
be glorified (12, 23), but this glory will spring from his
death as the ear of corn comes forth from the seed that
has perished in the ground (12, 24). It is in his death, too,
that the burning desire of the Good Shepherd will find
fulfilment: "I, when I am lifted up from the earth, will
draw all men to myself" (12, 32). After this, Jesus withdrew (12, 36b); the public ministry was at a close.

The evangelist, in his reflections on the ministry of
Jesus, is struck by the sad failure of the Jews to accept
their Messiah: "Though he had done so many signs in their
presence, yet they did not believe in him" (12, 37). He
rounds off the Book of Signs by an epilogue (12, 44-50)
where the leading ideas of the preceding chapters reoccur.
Jesus had clearly ended his ministry at 12, 36, and it
seems strange that he should begin to speak again in this
passage. We should recognize here a literary convention.
It is indeed a summary, and we should not be misled by
the use of direct speech for, in ancient writings, this style
is often employed where we would have indirect speech.
(See, for example, Mark 1, 14 f.; Acts 2, 40). It is
appropriate that the story of the ministry of our Lord
should end with a summary of his teaching.

The Supreme Manifestation of Christ

Our analysis of this third part of the gospel can be
rather brief, not, by any means, because it is of less importance, but simply because it is very much less involved
than the Book of Signs.

THE FAREWELL DISCOURSES (13-17).

Before the Passion-narrative St. John has given us a long discourse of our Lord, followed by a prayer. We are to take it that the discourse presents to us, rather in the style of Matthew, a synthesis of Christ's teaching. We do not doubt that our Lord did engage in intimate conversation with his disciples on the solemn occasion of the Last Supper, but we are justified in believing that the evangelist took advantage of this fact in order to give a fuller account of related teachings of his Master. When we examine the text, the truth of this observation is borne in on us. The sentence: "Rise, let us go hence" at the end of Chapter 14 is understandable only if the Passion-narrative were to follow immediately. It may be seen that Chapters 15 and 16 are, to a large extent, a repetition of Chapters 13 and 14; it would seem that Chapters 15 and 16 form a second version of the last discourse, or, perhaps, they are meant to complement it.

The washing of the feet (13, 1-11), which precedes the discourses, has been variously interpreted, but it seems best to regard it as symbolizing the great humiliation of the Passion. This incident is followed by the prediction of the betrayal by Judas, and his withdrawal (13, 21-30). The phrase "and it was night" (13, 30) is dramatic in the fashion of John—Judas is one of those who loves darkness rather than light (3, 19).

In Chapters 1-12 the leading ideas were "life" and "light," whereas in Chapter 13-17 these scarcely occur at all and the new theme is "love." With love are associated two other fundamental themes: consolation and union.[9] Jesus gives the supreme example of love, as the Good Shepherd laying down his life for his sheep. The disciples must love him as he loves them, and they must love one another because he loves each of them. He gives them only one commandment: "This is my command to you: love one another" (15, 17).

As he takes leave of his own, the Lord seeks to console them, and he gives them three grounds for consolation. They are not left as orphans, because he will come again to them (14, 3.18). He will send them another Advocate, a Consoler, who will remain with them and dwell in them

(14, 16). Above all he gives them the assurance that the Father will regard them with very special solicitude. It is the Father who will send the Paraclete (14, 16) and it is he who will grant whatever they ask in the name of Christ (16, 23); and all this for the reason that "the Father himself loves you, because you have loved me and believed that I came from God" (16, 27).

Finally, there is the theme of union: the union of Jesus and those who believe in him, in the allegory of the vine; the union of the disciples among themselves, in the concluding prayer. The followers of Christ are branches of that Vine planted by the Father himself; they live by the life of the Vine and, apart from him, they count for nothing and can do nothing (15, 1-8). The idea of unity is emphatically stressed in the prayer of Christ (Ch. 17). In the serene awareness that he has accomplished his work (17, 14) the great Priest of the new Alliance asks for the sanctification of his own. He is leaving them in the world and he prays that, closely linked together in love, they may be kept in the Father's name, preserved from evil and steadfast in the truth (17, 11-19). The prayer includes not only his immediate disciples but reaches out to all future believers (17, 20-26). He prays that all may be brought into the perfect unity of the divine life as shared by Father and Son.

Throughout these last discourses, though the setting is the eve of the Passion, yet, in a real sense, it is the glorified Lord who speaks—this is especially true of the final prayer. Thus, the Father has given all things into his hands (13, 3), has given him power over all flesh (17, 2): the prerogative of the Risen Christ (Matt. 28, 18). He has overcome the world (16, 33); he has finished the work that the Father has given him to do (17, 4); the Son of Man has been glorified (13, 21). Jesus can speak thus, within the atmosphere of fulfilment, because by his full acceptance of the will of his Father he was already glorified on the spiritual plane; but the death and resurrection remain yet to be accomplished on the historical plane. It is only on the Cross that he can finally say: It is accomplished (19, 30).

THE PASSION (18-19).

The story of the Passion as told by St. John is essentially the same as the synoptists' account—it is closest to Luke —but it also has some specifically Johannine differences. An interesting source of many of these differences is the fact that the Passion-narrative in John has many links with the Book of Signs. A study of some of these will, incidentally, shed much light on the evangelist's method.

Earlier in the gospel it had been pointed out that the Good Shepherd will lay down his life of his own accord (10, 18) and this is dramatized at the moment of arrest when, at the mere presence of Jesus, those who had come to take him became quite helpless (18, 6). Before giving himself up he insisted that his disciples should go free (18, 8-9) in order that the saying of his might be fulfilled: "I have not lost any of those whom you have given to me" (17, 12), which, in turn, refers back to 6, 37-40 and recalls, also, the words of the Shepherd: "No one will snatch them out of my hand" (10, 27-28). The Christ of John is always in full command of every situation and this characteristic is at its most striking in the Passion-narrative.

In 3, 14-15 we were told that the Son of Man must be "lifted up" and in 12, 32 Jesus declared: "When I am lifted up from the earth I shall draw all men to myself" and the evangelist notes that he said this in order to indicate the kind of death he was to die. The same comment is added when Jesus was transferred from the jurisdiction of the Sanhedrin to that of Pilate (18, 31-32). Now at last its meaning is clear: Jesus was not to die by stoning the Jewish method of execution—but, in accordance with Roman law, on a cross. For the evangelist that fact is highly significant: crucifixion is utterly humiliating—a criminal's death—and yet the victim on the cross is raised up towards heaven. "Thus, paradoxically in a sense and yet not illogically, the death of Christ is at once his descent and his ascent, his humiliation and his exaltation, his shame and his glory; and this truth is symbolized, for the evangelist, in the manner of his death—cruifixion, the most shameful death, which is, nevertheless, in a figure, his exaltation from the earth."[10]

In 9, 13-41 we have the theme of judgment treated with Johannine irony: the Pharisees sat in judgment upon the claims of Jesus and at the end found the tables turned and sentence pronounced against them. The situation is very much the same in the trial scene before Pilate. Jesus claimed that he had come to bear witness to the truth (18, 37), for he himself is the truth (14, 6). Truth and light are closely akin and it is the man that "does the truth" who alone can stand the scrutiny of the light (3, 21). Here the scornful question of Pilate: "What is truth?" (18, 38) marks him out as one who will not "come to the light" (3, 20). All the while it is Pilate who is being judged—this is explicit in 19, 11.

The evangelist gives as the last word of Jesus, before he bowed his head in death: "It is accomplished" (19, 30); the task is done. In 4, 34 we were told that his food is "to do the will of him who sent me and accomplish his work." In 5, 36 Jesus can point to a greater testimony than even the Baptist has rendered: "the works which the Father has given me to accomplish, these same works that I do, bear me witness." In his prayer to his Father he can already say: "I have glorified thee on earth by accomplishing the work which you gave me to do" (17, 4). At that moment Jesus had, in spirit, completed even the part of his task that yet remained, but on the Cross he can finally offer up that lifework with his life itself.

In 19, 34 f. the evangelist draws very special attention to the fact that, after the death of Christ on the Cross, water and blood issued from his side. The testimony is exceptionally solemn: "He who saw it bears witness—his testimony is true, and he knows that he speaks the truth —so that you too may believe." Here, if anywhere, we are surely invited to look for a deeper meaning. In Ch. 6 it was not stated how men can partake of the body and blood of Christ. Now it is also made clear that the wine at Cana is a sign of the blood of the true Vine; now we know that the sustenance of the eternal life which men receive depends on Christ's self-immolation in fulfilment of the will of God. In 7, 38 f. the water which will flow from the heart of Christ is explicitly said to symbolize the Spirit. At that stage the Spirit had not been given, because Jesus was not yet glorified; now at last "exalted" through the Cross, he can give that other great gift of God to men.

It now appears that the Passion is the great sign which gives meaning to all the others; yet it differs from all of them. The other signs, in themselves, even if they were miracles, had no lasting effect on history. The multitudes might eat of the loaves which Christ had provided for them, but they were soon hungry again. Unless they had "seen signs" the incident had no further relevance for them; it is the eternal reality that the event signified which really satisfies men's hunger. Lazarus was raised to life, but he must soon die again. The vital thing is what the raising signified: "He who lives and believes in me will never die." And so with the other signs; the Passion alone is different from all the others—the event of the Cross is unique.

"Here is something that happened in time with eternal consequence. Though individual men may miss its significance, nevertheless the thing has happened and history is different: the whole setting of human life in this world is different. It is an 'epoch-making' event; in history, things can never be the same again. But more: in it the two orders of reality, the temporal and the eternal, are united; the Word is made flesh. It is an event in both worlds; or rather, in that one world, of spirit and of flesh, which is the true environment of man, though he may fail to be aware of its twofold nature. Thus the cross is a sign, but a sign which is also the thing signified. The preliminary signs set forth so amply in the gospel are not only temporal signs of an eternal reality; they are also signs of this Event, in its twofold character as word and as flesh. They are true—spiritually, eternally true—only upon the condition that this Event is true, both temporally (or historically) and spiritually or eternally.'"[1]

It follows necessarily that, in this view, the story cannot end with the death of Jesus. His death on a cross, as we have seen, *signifies* his glorification and exaltation, but in reality it is the end of a struggle. What St. John sees is the deeper reality symbolized by the crucifixion: the death-and-resurrection as one complete event; that is why he can characterize the death of Christ as his "glorification." Consequently, he does not have to speak of the resurrection in itself (since in his view it is inseparable from the death of Jesus) and he is content to speak of some post-resurrection apparitions.

THE RISEN CHRIST (Ch. 20).

Quite like the Passion-narrative, the account of the post-Resurrection apparitions in John is very much the same as that of the Synoptics, yet with typically Johannine differences. We read, for instance, that the beloved disciple "saw and believed" when he entered the empty tomb—"for as yet they did not understand that, according to Scripture, he must rise from the dead" (20, 9). This observation, in some related form, is found at other points in the gospel: 2, 22; 16, 16. The meeting with Mary Magdalen is highly significant. Jesus tells her that she must not now touch him, cling to his feet, for he has not yet ascended to his Father. However, he is going to the Father without delay and he sends Mary to tell his brethren so.[12]

That same evening he came from the presence of his Father and appeared to his disciples. It is because he was now fully "glorified"—by his Death, Resurrection and Exaltation—that he can give them the gift of the Spirit (20, 22), for the Spirit was not, in fact, given until then (7, 39). Eight days later he appeared to them again, and this time Thomas was with them.

It is remarkable that in all these apparitions (and the same is true of Ch. 21) the Risen Christ is presented without any suggestion of divine majesty—such as is present in Matt. 28, 16-20. This procedure would seem to be closely linked to St John's doctrine that Christ is glorified and exalted in his death, for, by dying, Christ is really "going to the Father" (14, 28; 16, 10.16).[13] That is why he has consistently shown that the crucifixion, which is obviously an event on the historical plane, is, at the same time, and with more truth, an event on the spiritual plane, for this is the aspect of it that needs to be stressed. The resurrection, on the other hand, is first and foremost a reality on the spiritual plane, and the evangelist wants to show that it is also an event on the historical plane; that is why he stresses the reality of the post-resurrection appearances and, especially, Christ's renewal of personal relations with the disciples. Thus he shows that the death-and-resurrection, while retaining its full spiritual significance, is of vital importance for men precisely because it happened as a matter of history, at a point of time, in this world.

The solemn profession of faith by Thomas brings us to the meeting place of the temporal and spiritual worlds. It is the true climax of the gospel. Thomas sees the Jesus that he knew so well, he sees him in a given place and at a given time; but then he takes a step beyond place and time, into the realm of faith, into the eternal world. When he confesses Jesus as God he becomes one of those who has "seen his glory" (1, 14). The closing words of Jesus open up a vast perspective, for all men, to the end of time, who, like Thomas believe in this Lord and God, are included in the last solemn blessing: "Blessed are those who have not seen and yet believe" (20, 29). It is in order that these may, like Thomas, believe that Jesus is the Messiah, the Son of God, that this gospel has been written (20, 31).

APPENDIX: APPARITION BY THE LAKE (Ch. 21).

Chapter 21, though an appendix, is, at the same time a fitting postscript to the gospel, for it is concerned not immediately with Christ, as is the gospel, but with the Church which he left to carry on his work. The narrative of the miraculous draught of fishes (21, 1-14) symbolizes the conquests of that Church, founded on Peter (21, 15-17). The hyperbole of the conclusion (21, 25) is striking and effective, but though it is clearly an echo of the other, it lacks the marvellous solemnity and finality of 20, 30-31. It may be well to repeat the observation made earlier, that the fact of being an appendix does not derogate from the value of the last chapter of the gospel: it remains an essential part of the gospel.

XVII
Some Theological Ideas
of the Fourth Gospel

1. The Logos

The title of Logos (Word), which is applied to Jesus in the prologue of the fourth gospel, is found nowhere else in the New Testament except in the first epistle of St. John (1, 1) and in Apocalypse (19, 11-13). *Logos* is a Greek word of many meanings: it signifies not only the spoken word, but also the interior word of the mind—the thought or idea. Thus, our rendering "Word" does not fully translate the original term, which is wider, and can even designate the mind itself, as the faculty of thought.

In Greek philosophical speculation, especially within the Stoic system, the Logos represented a ruling principle, immanent in the world. This idea was adopted by the Alexandrian Jew, Philo—a contemporary of Christ—who set out to harmonize the Old Testament and the philosophy of his time. For him the Logos became an intermediary between God and the world, an instrument employed by God in the work of creation and in his dealings with the world. In his writings it can appear as an image of God and even as a divinity of lower rank.

St. John introduces the term Logos without explanation, and so intimates that it was familiar to his readers. It seems to have been, in fact, one of those vague philosophical terms that become common currency and are freely bandied about by people who may have very little acquaintance with philosophy. St. John makes the term the vehicle of his own ideas, which owe little to Greek speculation, and, most probably, very little to Philo either. It is not "Logos" but what John meant by it, that is important. Today it is almost universally recognized that the evangelist's thought is to be explained (if not entirely, at least predominantly) in terms of the Old Testament and of Christian tradition.

Logos is, naturally, a word of very frequent occurrence in the Greek Old Testament, and its use in two particular contexts is of special interest here.[1] In one group of passages the Word of God is creative, for instance in the creation story (Gen. 1, 3.6.9)—summarized in Ps. 33, 6: "By the word of the Lord were the heavens made." In another group of passages the "word of God" is that spoken by the prophets, the word of revelation (e.g., Am. 3, 1; Jer. 1, 4; Ez. 1, 3). It is significant that the ideas of creation and revelation are in evidence in the prologue of John (1, 3; 1, 18) and it is surely reasonable to see here the influence of the Old Testament.

Another very important Old Testament concept, which must also inevitably lie behind John's use of Logos, is that of divine Wisdom. We should recall that *Logos* signifies not only the spoken word, but also the thought. This Wisdom was with God "before he made anything from the beginning" (Prov. 8, 22); it is "the brightness of eternal light, the unspotted mirror of God's majesty and the image of his goodness" (Wisd. 7, 26). The divine Wisdom is very often personified and, by a literary device, is described as a personal being, standing by the side of God, and bearing some relation to the created world. As such, Wisdom appears as a foreshadowing of the Word of John and must have been immediately present to the evangelist's mind.

In Jewish thought the Law was the Word of God, *par excellence,* and the rabbis often personified the Law. Here, too, we can reasonably hope to find part of the background of the Johannine Word, if only by contrast. For it does seem clear that John sets up an opposition between his Word and the Word of the Law: "The Law was given through Moses; grace and truth came through Jesus Christ" (1, 17)—who is the true Word of God.

The Christian background is certainly not less important than the Jewish. In the New Testament the word of God is frequently the message of salvation, the gospel (Luke 8, 11; II Tim. 2, 9; Apoc. 1, 9; I John 1, 1). It was spoken by Paul (Acts 13, 5; I Thess. 2, 13) and by the other Apostles (Acts 6, 2) and by Jesus himself (Luke 5, 1; Mark 2, 2). But the gospel that Paul and the Apostles preached was in reality Christ (I Cor. 1, 23; Gal. 3, 1; Acts 2, 36; 4, 12). It is on the person of Jesus that St. John, too, focuses his attention; he sees very clearly that Jesus is himself the message of salvation, the Word.

It would seem to follow that though Logos is a Greek term, and may possibly have been chosen as a concession to Greek mentality, yet the sources of St. John's thought are altogether Jewish and Christian; and it follows, too, that the Prologue is quite in line with the rest of the gospel. John teaches that the Logos exists from eternity, that he is with God from eternity, that he is God and the creator of all things. Lastly, and most wonderfully, he teaches that this Word "was made flesh." For it is in the person of Jesus alone that the pre-existing Logos is made known to men; and though the title "Logos" does not appear in the rest of the gospel, yet the gospel itself is comprehensible only in the light of the conviction that Jesus is the Incarnate Word.

2. Christ in the Fourth Gospel

Jesus is, and must be, the center of all the gospels, but the fourth gospel is focused on him exclusively. In general, too, the Synoptic gospels are theologically less developed than the fourth gospel—they are more dependent on the apostolic preaching, on the primitive catechesis. John is the result of meditation, Spirit-guided, on the works and words of Jesus, and it presents the strongly personal view of its author. In the Synoptics the progression in Christ's self-revelation is still traceable, but the fourth gospel presents Jesus, from its opening words, as the Logos, the only-begotten Son.

In the first three gospels we can regard Jesus through the eyes of his contemporaries and see only a man, though a man shrouded in mystery. In John we cannot, for a moment, close our eyes to the divinity of Christ. This gospel is dominated by the statement: "The Word was made flesh," and it is God-made-Man who stands out in every episode of it. The Jesus who sat, wearied from his journey, by Jacob's well (4, 6) cannot hide the fact that he is the Messiah and the Savior of the world (4, 29.42). At his mere presence those who have come to arrest him are helpless (18, 6). In the trial-scene, before Pilate, the Prisoner is serenely in command of the situation (18, 37; 19, 11). He died only when he was sure that his work had been accomplished, because he had power to lay down his life—that he might take it up again (19, 28-30; 10, 18). Indeed, the very purpose of the gospel is to bring home to its readers the twofold aspect of the Incarnation, the mystery of the historical and human figure who is, nevertheless, divine: "These are written that you may believe that *Jesus* is the Christ, the *Son of God*" (20, 31).

The fundamental theme of the gospel, indicated in the prologue, may be framed as follows: "The only Son of God has become man and has been sent into the world by the Father in order to reveal to men the riches of the divine life and to communicate to them that same life."[2] In view of this, the emphasis is on the Incarnation of Christ rather than on the mysteries of his Death and Resurrection. But it is a question of emphasis only because for St. John (no less than for Paul) it is indeed by his death and resurrection that Christ saves us—that is his "hour" *par excellence.* Yet it remains true that the fourth evangelist does visualize the Incarnation as being already, in itself, the mystery of salvation. So, for instance, the prologue concentrates on it and does not mention Calvary and the resurrection.

We can effectively study St. John's approach to the Incarnation by examining the formulas used by Jesus in this gospel to describe himself. Thus he speaks of himself as the one *sent by the Father*. This idea is not absent from the earliest Christian teaching, but it recurs constantly throughout the fourth gospel and is distinctive of it. The title *Son of Man* is found quite often in the Synoptics, and we have studied its use in Mark.[3] In John we find that the idea of Son of Man is set in close relation to the ideas of *exaltation* and *glorification*.[4] Referring to Num. 21, 4-9 Jesus declared: "As Moses lifted up the serpent in the desert, so must the Son of Man be lifted up" (3, 14). In discussion with the Jews he affirmed: "When you have lifted up the Son of Man, then you will know that I am" (8, 28). Shortly before his Passion he opened a discourse on the Son of Man with the words: "The hour has come for the Son of Man to be glorified . . . Father, glorify thy name." And he continued: "Now shall the ruler of this world be cast out, and I, when I am lifted up from the earth, will draw all men to myself" (12, 23-32). In this last passage the two perspectives, of exaltation and of glorification, are evidently associated. Later, at the beginning of the discourse after the Supper, when Judas had departed to betray him, he declared again: "Now is the Son of Man glorified, and God is glorified in him" (13, 31).

Elevation and glorification are two complementary aspects of the same reality. The death of Jesus on a cross is symbolic of his elevation (12, 33) because his death is only the first step towards a higher elevation, the exaltation to the right hand of God. There the Son of Man will be clothed in the divine glory, for when Christ ascends to the presence of God he finds again that glory which had been his eternally: "Now, Father, glorify me with the glory which I had with thee before the world was made" (17, 5). This Son of Man has, indeed, descended from heaven (3, 13; 6, 33.38.41.50.51.58) and he must return to heaven, his true fatherland, to be glorified there (3, 14; 6, 62; 8, 28; 12, 24-33; 13, 31). That is why, in John, exaltation and glorification are proper to the Son of Man: it is because he is heavenly, and has come from heaven, that he must, one day, be "elevated" and "glorified" at the right hand of God.

In the Synoptics Jesus is called *Son of God*,[5] but in

John that title is used more frequently, and in almost all cases is taken in the strict sense of natural divine sonship (e.g., 3, 35; 5, 17; 10, 30.38; 14, 11.20; 17, 10). Yet there is something specifically Johannine about the title, for, though there is perfect communion between Father and Son (5, 19.20-23; 10, 14-15; 12, 28; 13, 31-32; 17, 1.4.5.12) yet, at the same time, in Christ's declarations, there is a remarkable attitude of submission to the Father (e.g., 5, 30; 8, 26.38.40; 14, 10; 15, 10). That is because, in this gospel, Jesus always speaks in his historical situation as *incarnate* Son of God.

Of very great importance in the self-revelation of Jesus are the formulas beginning "I am." *I am* the bread of life come down from heaven (6, 35.41.48.51), the light of the world (8, 12; 9, 5), the door of the sheep (10, 7-9), the good shepherd (10, 11.14), the resurrection and the life (11, 25), the way, the truth and the life (14, 6), the true vine (15, 1.5). It is the absolute use of the term (8, 24.28.58; 13, 19), already noted, that gives the key to its full significance, for these verses refer directly to the revelation of the divine Name made to Moses (Ex. 3, 13.15). In all cases where the solemn "I am" occurs it is the divine Son of God who speaks.

The incarnate Son reveals to men the mystery of the divine life, and communicates that life to them; so the notion of life occupies a leading place in the fourth gospel. Life is a property of God, but the incarnation of the Son of God indicates a descent of the divine life into this corruptible world; for just as the Father has life in himself so he has granted to the incarnate Son to have life in himself; and the Son, in his turn, gives life to whom he wills—he gives living water, he is the bread of life. The life that he gives is divine not alone because of its origin, but by its very nature; it is the same eternal life communicated to him by the Father.

This life the believer possesses here and now, for he who believes in Jesus has already passed from death to life (5, 24). Natural death will in no way interrupt the union with Christ who is resurrection and life (11, 23-25) and he who eats the bread of life has eternal life and is as-

sured of bodily resurrection (6, 54). The allegory of the
vine (15, 1-8) graphically illustrates the reality of the
current of life which flows from Jesus to the disciples,
because, in the thought of St. John, the union of vine and
branches is only a pale shadow of the supreme union
within the true Vine.

Christ himself is the fullness of life and light, and like
light, life is a positive perfection.[6] Accordingly, in the
fourth gospel, Jesus is more Savior than Redeemer. Once
again it is a matter of emphasis; St. John does not deny
that Jesus has redeemed us from our sins (cf. 1, 29), but
he does not insist on this. He views the world in a detached
way, from above. He is aware of sin, but he sees it as a lack
of something, the non-possession of the life that is in Christ.
He makes this point, with a clarity that is disconcerting,
in his first epistle: "He who has the Son has life; he who
has not the Son has not life" (I John 5, 12). This statement,
so simple and yet so profound, epitomizes the outlook of
St. John and his most earnest conviction; it explains why
his gospel is centered so utterly on the Son of God.

3. Baptism and Eucharist in John

Nowhere else in the New Testament do the two
great sacraments of Baptism and the Eucharist figure quite
so largely as in John; yet, the remarkable fact is that, unlike the Synoptics, we are given no account of the institution of the Eucharist and no specific command to baptize.
St. John is writing for Christians who are acquainted with
the sacramental system, and his interest is in the *theology*
of the sacraments. His main teaching on the Eucharist is
given in the discourse at Capharnaum (Ch. 6) where Jesus
explains the necessity of eating the true bread from heaven,
and indicates, for those who will hear and understand, the
meaning of that intimate communion with him. In the
discourse wth Nicodemus (Ch. 3) Baptism is shown to
be a rebirth from above through water and the Spirit.

In the two chapters mentioned, the sacraments are
treated specifically, but the evangelist's interest in Baptism
and the Eucharist runs through the gospel.[7] The baptism
of John is explicitly contrasted with the baptism of Jesus:

"he who sent me to baptize with water said to me . . . 'this is he who baptizes with water and the Holy Spirit'" (1, 33). At Cana the wine has, at least secondarily, a eucharistic significance. The "living water" of Ch. 4—which in 7, 37-39 is said to symbolize the Spirit—would spontaneously remind a Christian reader of Baptism. The narrative of the blind man who regained his sight when he was sent by Christ, the light of the world and the life-giver, to wash in the pool of Siloam, cannot fail to be regarded as an intentional reference to that other miracle which takes place in each baptism.

The allegory of the vine in Ch. 15 would seem to have a eucharistic significance. The passage is the complement of Ch. 6, for the statement "I am the true vine" balances the other: "I am the bread of life" (6, 35). In both places—the mention of Judas (6, 70) and the greater love that leads to the laying down of life (15, 13)—the death of Jesus is in view, and the Eucharist is indissolubly linked to the death of Christ (I Cor. 11-26). The union between the branches and the vine is, above all, the eucharistic communion of Christians with Christ. Finally, in 19, 34 the blood and water flowing from the side of the dead Christ (a fact so solemnly attested 19, 35) symbolize beyond any doubt the two sacraments. Now when Jesus was glorified he could give the Spirit, and give, too, his flesh and blood to be the food of the faithful.

This last passage is of the greatest importance. In it the two sacraments of Baptism and Eucharist are shown to be bound in the closest way to the death of Jèsus. They spring out of his sacrifice of love and atonement, and are linked to his humanity. But if the Lord instituted these sacraments during his life, and if they are bound so closely to his death, they are no less closely related to the risen and ascended Christ. It is only when he had ascended to the Father that he could send the Spirit (7, 39; 20, 17) and it is in the Spirit that he communicates his presence, both in Baptism (3, 5) and in the Eucharist (6, 63).

St. John's interest in Baptism and the Eucharist is really only another aspect of his all-consuming interest in Christ. He stresses them so much because he sees that they are the fulfilment of the promise of Jesus that he would not abandon his disciples (14, 18). By Baptism each Christian is joined to the Risen Lord, and in the Eucharist the Risen Christ lives on in the Christian community. The person of Jesus has taken the place of the Temple (2, 21-22) and the true worship is worship in the Spirit (4, 23). The Word who became flesh and dwelt among men abides among his own forever.

Notes and References

Reference to evangelists and gospels

In order to distinguish clearly between references to an evangelist and to a gospel, the following system has been followed:

The *evangelist* will always be: St. Matthew, St. Mark, St. Luke, St. John.

The *gospel* will always be: Matthew, Mark, Luke, John.

In references to any particular verse or verses of the gospels (or of any of the books of the Bible) the accepted method will be used. E.g.,

Matt. 2, 3 = Chapter 2 of Matthew, verse 3.

Luke 14, 8 f = Chapter 14 of Luke, verse 8 and the following verse.

Mark 4, 1-9 = the whole passage from verse 1 to verse 9 inclusive, of Mark chapter 4.

Chapter 1

1. An unidentified feast (5, 1) may possibly be another Pasch, thus giving a ministry of over three years; at any rate it lasted considerably longer than one year.

2. Matthew and Luke go back to the birth of our Lord but the primitive preaching began with the Baptist and the baptism of Jesus. It was later that interest in the human origin of the Son of God gave rise to the Infancy narratives.

3. The translation of all New Testament passages is made directly from the Greek text. In some few cases, as here, it is very literal in order to illustrate the point at issue.

4. P. Benoit, O. P., *Revue Biblique*, 1946, p. 501.

Chapter II

1. From now on the term "Synoptics" and "synoptical" will be used to designate the first three gospels and matters relating to them.

2. "Children of the wedding-feast" or "of the bride-chamber" is a Semitic idiom for the companions of the bridegroom, or simply, for the wedding guests.

3. The theory outlined here is that proposed by L. Vaganay in *Le Problème Synoptique*, Paris, 1954—he is careful to point out that he does not present it as a final solution to the problem. It would not be true to say that Vaganay's hypothesis has won anything like universal acceptance, but it has been very favorably received by such eminent scholars as Msgr. L. Cerfaux of Louvain, and P. Benoit who has incorporated it in the *Bible de Jérusalem*. It not only marks a healthy reaction against an over-simplified approach to what is essentially a complicated problem, but it is also a definite step in the direction of a solution. Whatever the fate of the theory will be, *Le Problème Synoptique* is certainly one of the most significant works on the subject.

4. Our gospel of Matthew is not just one of these versions; it is more than a mere translation of the Aramaic gospel, as we shall see. "Matthew" will always refer to the gospel as we know it—any reference to the Aramaic gospel will be explicit.

5. Though Mark is the earliest of the gospels in the form in which they are known to us, yet, for purposes of reference, the traditional order is always followed. Thus, the "first gospel" = Matthew; the "second gospel" = Mark; the "third gospel" = Luke; the "fourth gospel" = John.

Chapter IV

1. For what that investigation will show us we shall again draw on Vaganay, as he sets out the matter in its context of the "Synoptic Problem." See above, p. 20

2. Though "Hebrew" or the "language of the Hebrews" are the expressions used in these testimonies, there is no doubt that Aramaic is meant. Hebrew was no longer spoken at this time and the current Aramaic was, by non-Jewish Christians, loosely termed "Hebrew."

3. There is, obviously, room for confusion between the Greek and Aramaic gospels, but that confusion can be avoided, at least in this work, if it is kept in mind that "Matthew" will always stand for the Greek gospel—the gospel as we know it—

whereas any reference to the Aramaic gospel will be quite explicit.

4. A. Wikenhauser, *Einleitung in das Neue Testament*, Freiburg, 1956,² p. 144.

Cf J. Schmid, *Das Evangelium nach Matthäus*, Regensburg, 1956² p. 31.

Chapter V

1. The plan here followed is that given by Father P. Benoit, O.P. in the *Bible de Jérusalem*.

2. L. Vaganay, *Le Problème Synoptique*, pp. 200-201.

3. "Eschatological" comes from the Greek *eschata* = the last things. Eschatology is teaching concerning the last things—the close of this present age and the end of the world. This discourse of our Lord on the destruction of Jerusalem, the second coming of the Messiah and the general judgment (Matt. 24-25) is known as the "eschatological discourse."

4. P. Benoit, op. cit., p. 1287.

5. J. Dupont, O.S.B., *Les Béatitudes*, Bruges, 1959, pp. 43-204.

I am entirely indebted to this brilliant study for the following analysis of the Sermon.

6. The very close parallelism between these passages is remarkable:

Matt. 6, 2-4.	6, 5-6.	6, 6-18.
When, therefore you give alms, sound no trumpet	And when you pray,	When you fast, do not look dismal
before you as the hypocrites do	you must not be like the hypocrites	as the hypocrites do
	for they love to stand and pray	for they disfigure their faces
in the synagogues and in the streets	in the synagogues and at the street corners that they	
That they may be honored by men.	may be seen by men.	that they may be seen by men to fast.
Amen, I say to you,	Amen, I say to you,	Amen, I say to you,
they have already	they have already	they have already

received their reward.	received their reward.	received their reward.
As for you, when you give alms, do not let your left hand know what your right hand is doing, so that your alms	As for you, when you pray, retire to your room and shut the door, and pray to	As for you, when you fast, anoint your head and wash your face, so that your fasting may not be seen by men, but by
	your Father,	your Father,
may be in secret;	who is there, in secret;	who is there, in secret;
and your Father, who sees in secret, will reward you.	and your Father, who sees in secret, will reward you.	and your Father, who sees in secret, will reward you.

7. Op. cit., p. 204.

8. Aramaisms are turns of speech that, though found in the Greek text of the gospel, are really Aramaic idiom. A similar phenomenon can be found outside the gospels. How many Irish people, for instance, advert to the fact that the widely used expression: "I am just after coming" is pure Irish idiom (Táim díreach taréis teacht)?

9. M.-J. Lagrange, O.P., *Evangile selon St Matthieu*, Paris, 1923, p. 1.

Chapter VI

1. In Matt. 5, 21-48 we find six comparisons between a command of the old Law and the demands of our Lord. "You have heard that it was said to the men of old (i.e., said in the Old Testament to the Jews): 'Thou shalt not kill' . . . But I say to you: 'Thou shalt not be angry with thy brother'" (5, 21-22). The remaining five follow the same pattern and in each case it is clear that our Lord, far from abolishing the command of the Old Law, demands that it be observed much more perfectly. In his version of the Sermon on the Mount St. Luke does not have these "antitheses." The reason is obvious: the contract between the old Law and the new is of little interest to Gentiles, who do not know the old Law; but for Matthew's Jewish readers it was of vital importance.

2. Yahweh, sometimes wrongly written "Jehovah," is the

special name for God in the Old Testament. Because of the Jewish scruple indicated above, it was not pronounced when the Scriptures were read aloud—the word *Adonai* = "Lord" was substituted for it. In most translations of the Old Testament Yahweh is always rendered by "the Lord," but certain modern versions, notably the outstanding *Bible de Jérusalem*, rightly reproduce the original "Yahweh."

3. A. Feuillet, *Introduction à la Bible II*, Tournai, 1959, pp. 800-818. I am very deeply indebted to this fine study for the following treatment of the Church seen as the actualization of the Kingdom of God. I might add, apropos of the work cited, that the exposition of major themes of the New Testament, by A. Feuillet and S. Lyonnet, is the highlight of what is easily the best Catholic Introduction to the New Testament.

4. A. Feuillet, op. cit., p. 805.

5. P. Benoit, *L'Evangile Selon saint Matthieu* (BJ), Paris, 1953, pp. 103-104.

6. P. Benoit, *Bible de Jérusalem*, Paris, 1956, p. 1311.

7. In Matt. 16, 16 the declaration of Peter runs: "You are the Christ, the Son of the living God." But Mark has: "You are the Christ" (8, 29) and Luke (9. 20): "The Christ of God." Some have understood the words of Peter (in Matthew) as referring to the divine Sonship of Christ. But in view of Mark ("Christ" is the Greek translation of "Messiah") and of the general lack of understanding on the part of the disciples, it is better to take them as referring to his Messianic dignity. Besides, Peter's rebuke to our Lord, immediately after the confession (16, 22) is scarcely compatible with an acknowledgement of his divinity. We shall see (when we study Mark) how very difficult it was for the disciples to grasp Christ's notion of spiritual Messiahship, and Peter would certainly have required a divine revelation if he were to accept it (16, 17). The full title employed by Matthew does not, *of itself*, go beyond the Messianic significance, but it is certain that the evangelist, *when he wrote the gospel*—and therefore in the light of his post-Resurrection faith—had in mind the divine Sonship in the strict sense. This distinction, between the disciples' very imperfect understanding of Jesus, and their enlightened faith in the Risen Lord, is certainly a valid one and should be kept in mind when reading the gospels.

Chapter VII

1. Papias got his information from "John the Elder"—who

is not John the Apostle; though he was clearly a man of the first Christian generation. See Part I, p. 30.

2. See L. Vaganay, *Le Problème Synoptique,* Tournai 1952, pp. 52-53. 154-156.

3. The "Anti-Marcionite Prologues" were prefaces attached to the gospels (and many of the epistles) to defend their authenticity against the attacks of the heretic Marcion, who accepted as canonical (i.e., as Scripture) only Luke and ten epistles of St. Paul. The beginning of the Prologue to Mark has not been preserved.

4. Vincent Taylor, *The Gospel According to St. Mark,* London, 1953, p. 26.

5. L. Vaganay, op. cit., pp. 152-154.

6. It is widely accepted that the "young man" mentioned in Mark 14, 51-52 is the evangelist; otherwise it is not easy to understand why the incident should have been mentioned.

Chapter VIII

1. This plan is based on the one given by V. Taylor, op. cit., pp. 107-111.

2. See p. 14.

3. M.-J. Lagrange, O.P., *Évangile selon saint Marc,* Paris 1929, p. lxiv.

4. Op. cit., pp. 156-174. See pp. 30-33.

5. J. Huby, S.J.—X. Léon-Dufour, S.J., *L'Évangile et les Évangiles,* Paris 1954, pp. 156-158.

6. See pp. 30-33.

7. L. Vaganay, op. cit., pp. 44-45.

8. V. Taylor, op. cit., pp. 78-104. See X. Léon-Dufour, *Introduction à la Bible,* Tournai 1959, pp. 207-208.

9. See p. 22.

10. X. Léon-Dufour, op. cit., p. 202.

11. See pp. 14-15.

12. Aramaisms are turns of speech which, though found in the Greek text of the gospel, are really Aramaic idiom.

13. A. Wikenhauser, *Einleitung in das Neue Testament,* Freiburg (1956²) p. 121.

14. V. Taylor, op. cit., p. 105.

15. L. Vaganay, *Revue Biblique,* 1951, pp. 5-46.

16. See J. Huby—X. Léon-Dufour, op. cit., 145-151.

17. The translation of Mark 5, 21-43 is deliberately rather literal, and gives an idea of the style of Mark. The monotonous linking of sentences, and phrases, by the conjunction "and" is quite apparent. With regard to the other texts, the dependence

of Luke on Mark is manifest, whereas Matthew has a much simpler and more stylized version.

18. V. Taylor, op. cit., pp. 148-149.

Chapter IX

1. See, however, pp. 62-65.

2. P. Benoit, O.P., *Exégèse et Théologie* I, Paris 1961, p. 136. This is the reprint of an article on the divinity of Jesus in the Synoptics, which first appeared in *Lumière et Vie*, no. 9, 1953. That number of *Lumière et Vie* is now available in English translation as: *Son and Saviour: The Divinity of Jesus Christ in the Scriptures*, Geoffrey Chapman, London 1960.

3. The title "Son of Man" in a Messianic sense occurs in the Jewish apocryphal *Book of Enoch* of the first century B.C. It is found in the "Similitudes" section of the book, Chs. 37-71. Fragments of several Mss. of *Enoch* have been found in cave 4 at Qumran (the place of origin of the "Dead Sea Scrolls"), but the "Similitudes" section is not represented. According to Father J. T. Milik (one of the foremost authorities on the Scrolls) this fact is highly significant and gives strong support to the position of many scholars who had already regarded this part of the book as a Christian interpolation. In that case *Enoch* ceases to provide an argument for the Jewish Messianic interpretation of "Son of man." See J. T. Milik, *Ten Years of Discovery in the Wilderness of Judaea*, SCM Press, London, 1959, pp. 33-34. It is nevertheless probable that in certain restricted circles of pious Jews the Messiah was seen as the Son of man. See P. Benoit, op. cit., pp. 137-138.

4. Translation: E. J. Kissane, *The Book of Isaiah* II, Dublin 1943, pp. 181-182.

5. A. Feuillet, *Introduction à la Bible* II, p. 792.

6. See W. Harrington, O.P., *Doctrine and Life*, 1959, pp. 61-67.

7. It must be admitted that the warnings to preserve silence, as found in Mark, are to some extent artificial, stereotyped. Sometimes silence is imposed when its observance is impossible, e.g., at the raising of the daughter of Jairus (5, 21-43) and at the healing of the deaf-mute (7, 36f) and of the blind man (8, 26). In these cases we perceive the influence of the faith of the early Church, a faith which now saw that the reality of the person of Jesus would not be fully known until after the Resurrection. This is not to say that St. Mark, moved by this faith, invented the Messianic Secret; but it does mean that we saw it loom behind the whole work of Christ.

See J. Schmid, *Das Evangelium nach Markus*, Regensburg (1954²) pp. 158-159.

8. P. Benoit, op. cit., p. 141.

9. *Ibid*, 1. c.

Chapter X

1. The Muratorian canon is a list of the inspired books which were accepted by the Roman Church about the end of the second century. The list, which is fragmentary, takes its name from the fact that it was discovered in the Ambrosian Library, Milan, by the Italian scholar Muratori, and was published by him in 1740.

2. A. Wikenhauser, *Einleitung in das Neue Testament*, p. 161.

3. *Évangile selon Saint Luc*, Paris 1921, p. cxl.

4. See A. Wikenhauser, op. cit., pp. 161-162.

J. Schmid, *Das Evangelium nach Lukas*, Regensburg (1955²) p. 26.

5. X. Léon-Dufour, *Introduction à la Bible* II, p. 257.

Chapter XI

1. X. Léon-Dufour, op. cit., p. 233.

2. See p. 31.

3. Ibid.

4. L. Vaganay, *Le Problème Synoptique*, pp. 112-126.

5. P. Benoit, *Bible de Jérusalem*, p. 1352.

6. *The Gospel of Jesus Christ*, I, London, 1950, p. 10.

7. L. Vaganay, op. cit., pp. 263-264.

8. P. Benoit, op. cit., p. 1289.

9. R. Laurentin, *Structure et Théologie de Luc 1-2* (Études Bibliques), Paris 1957, pp. 32-33.

10. J. Dupont, O.S.B., *Les Béatitudes*, Bruges 1958, pp. 43-204.

11. See pp. 104-105.

12. The "antitheses" are found in Matt. 5, 21-48. They are so named because the new Law, formulated by Christ, is contrasted with the precepts of the Old Law. This contrast is explicit in each of the six antitheses: E. g. "You have heard that it was said (in the Law): 'Thou shalt not kill . . .' But I say to you: 'Thou shalt not be angry . . .' "—Similarly with the others.

13. X. Léon-Dufour, op. cit., pp. 238-240.

14. *Évangile selon Saint Luc*, p. xxxviii.

Chapter XII

1. There are no grounds for identifying the anonymous woman (whom St. Luke courteously refrains from naming) with Mary Magdalen (8, 2), and still less with Mary the sister of Martha (10, 38-42). The evangelist has obviously indicated three different women.

2. M.-J. Lagrange, *The Gospel of Jesus Christ* I, p. 24.

3. *Évangile selon Saint Luc*, p. xlvii.

4. J. Schmid, op. cit., p. 108.

5. M. J. Lagrange, op. cit., pp. xlv-xlvi.

Chapter XIII

1. C. K. Barrett, *The Gospel According to St. John* S.P.C.K., London 1955, p. 87.

2. A. Feuillet, *Introduction à la Bible II*, Tournai 1959, pp. 651-652.

3. M.-E. Boismard, *Bible de Jérusalem*, Paris 1956, p. 1396.

4. A. Wikenhauser, *Einleitung in das Neue Testament*, Freiburg 1956², pp. 208-210.

5. A. Wikenhauser, op. cit., pp. 221-222.

Chapter XIV

1. M.-E. Boismard, *Du Baptéme à Cana* (Lectio Divina), Paris 1956, p. 7.

2. See pp. 34-37.

3. W. Grossouw, *Revelation and Redemption*, Geoffrey Chapman, London 1958, pp. 11-17.
This little book, an introduction to the theology of John, can be very warmly recommended. It will be found most helpful by anyone wishing to understand the fourth gospel.

4. C. Spicq, *Revue Biblique*, 1958, p. 363.

5. C. K. Barrett, op. cit., pp. 18-21.

6. *The Interpretation of the Fourth Gospel*, C.U.P. 1955, p. 290. See A. Feuillet, op. cit., pp. 640-643.
I feel that any displacement theory must first of all reckon with Professor Dodd's impressive case, on theological grounds, for the unity of the gospel. It seems to me that his position is very strong indeed.

7. Op. cit., p. 219.

8. M.-J. Lagrange, *Evangile selon saint Jean*, Paris 1925, p. 222. See p. 85.

9. See M.-J. Lagrange, op. cit., P. 135.

He, however, accepts v. 3b as authentic—but the growing tendency is to exclude it also.

10. Op. cit., p. 217.

11. See pp. 16-17.

12. See pp. 103-107.

13. See pp. 14-15.

14. We cannot, even in view of limited space, pass over altogether in silence the relationship between John and the Qumran texts. Among the manuscripts found at Qumran—the Dead Sea Scrolls—there are some that have shed light on the New Testament. It is notably with John and the epistles of St. Paul that the greatest number of points of contact, both literary and doctrinal, have been discovered. Both John (and Paul) and the Qumran sectarians were influenced by currents of thought that were prevalent in certain circles of Judaism at that time. In John a form of dualism is expressed in contrasts: light-darkness, truth-falsehood, life-death. The evangelist treats light, truth and life as kindred and often identical images, and the same holds good for darkness, falsehood and death. The meaning of these expressions is very close to that of similar ones in the Qumran texts, where they occur a number of times in practically the same sense. In these texts, too, stress is laid on a spirit of unity in fraternal love.

Such ideas are frequent in John, but with notable differences. Thus the fraternal love so insisted upon in Qumran is limited to members of the sect; all other men are hated as enemies of God. This is not Christian charity. It is the word "Christian" indeed that underlines the essential difference between the Scrolls and the gospel. The occurrence of these various themes in the fourth gospel and in the Qumran writings points to a common Jewish background, but in John these same ideas have been quite transformed by the impact of Christian revelation and Christian faith. One positive result of these contacts is to emphasize further the essential Jewish background of the fourth gospel.

Chapter XV

1. See Oscar Cullmann, *Early Christian Worship*, SCM Press 1953, pp. 50-56.

2. Op. cit., pp. 22-23.

3. *Revue Biblique*, 1946, p. 501.

4. It seems that we should accept John's dating of the event. Since the synoptists have, artificially, condensed the ministry of our Lord into one year, and have allowed for only

one journey to Jerusalem, they had no choice but to place the clearing of the Temple in the context of that visit. See M.-J. Lagrange, op. cit., pp. 64-65.

Chapter XVI

1. See C. H. Dodd, op. cit., pp. 289-443. Throughout this chapter I am constantly in the debt of the eminent Cambridge scholar. See A. Feuillet, op. cit., pp. 626-638.

2. In John 1, 34 instead of "Son of God" some important Mss. have "Elect of God," and this reading is accepted as the better one by a great number of scholars.

3. M.-E. Boismard, *Du Baptéme à Cana*, pp. 56-57.

4. A. Feuillet, op. cit., p. 630.

5. See above, p. 15.

6. R. H. Lightfoot, *St. John's Gospel*, Oxford 1956, p. 9.

7. C. H. Dodd, op. cit., pp. 344-345. See A. Feuillet, op. cit., p. 631.

8. P. Benoit, *Exégèse et Théologie I*, Paris 1961, p. 389.

9. A. Feuillet, op. cit., p. 636.

10. C. H. Dodd, op. cit., p. 435.

11. Ibid., p. 439.

12. P. Benoit, *Revue Biblique* 1949, pp. 161-203. See A. Wikenhauser, *Die Apostel-Geschichte*, Regensburg 1956,[2] pp. 28-32.

It is clear that, according to the New Testament itself and early ecclesiastical tradition, our Lord went to his Father on Easter Sunday. The Ascension forty days later (mentioned by St. Luke in Acts 1, 6-11) is the final leave-taking of Christ—now he will no longer come from the presence of his Father to appear to his disciples as he did during the short time after the Resurrection. It should be made clear that though the liturgical feast of Ascension Day commemorates this final Ascension only, it is in no way opposed to the other tradition. In the course of time the emphasis fell altogether on this final Ascension and the other aspect of the mystery was lost sight of. A close parallel is provided by the Resurrection. Though the Fourth Gospel and St. Paul stress the paramount importance of the Resurrection yet, in the course of centuries, it was gradually relegated to a very secondary place in our theology. Now, quite recently, the restored Paschal liturgy has rectified this and the Resurrection is once again seen to be central, theologically as well as liturgically.

13. C. H. Dodd, op. cit., pp. 441-442.

Chapter XVII

1. C. K. Barrett, op. cit., pp. 127-130.
2. A. Feuillet, op. cit., p. 890.
3. See p. 88.
4. M.-E. Boismard, op. cit., pp. 108-112.
5. See pp. 63-65.
6. W. Grossouw, op. cit., pp. 89-91.
7. See O. Cullmann, op. cit., pp. 37-119.